Praise for *How to Be Fine*

"Read this book, take a bre... Kristen are so forthright, f... but be won over by them. I... practical advice here that can help y...

—Celeste Headlee, host of *Retro Report* on
PBS and author of *We Need to Talk*

"[A] grounded, large-hearted work. . . . Greenberg and Meinzer craft a welcoming tone and strike a perfect balance between sharing their traumas and folding in amusing anecdotes. This will delight fans of self-help books and encourage even the hardest cynics to reconsider the genre."

—*Publishers Weekly*

"Jolenta and Kristen are the mythbusters, guinea pigs, and guides you can trust to sort the Big Self-Help trash from treasure. Now they've created a hilariously relatable how-to for navigating the sprawling world of self-help and trends with equal parts hope and skepticism. Whether you're looking for an entertaining route through the genre, or just reassurance that you're not the only one who falls apart sometimes, *How to Be Fine* will make you feel better."

— Caroline Ervin and Cristen Conger, founders of
Unladylike Media and authors of *Unladylike: A Field Guide
to Smashing the Patriarchy and Claiming Your Space*

"Calling all skeptics and true believers—Jolenta and Kristen live and learn so we don't have to! Seriously, they are the dreamiest tour guides one could have on a self-help journey. So much humor, heart, and honesty throughout—you'll be rewarded with tons of concrete tips and heart-stopping moments of genuine soul-searching."

—Michele Siegel, producer of the podcasts Magic
Lessons with Elizabeth Gilbert and Dear Sugars

"I've long been a huge fan of Jolenta and Kristen's podcast By the Book, a sharp, hilarious, and intersectional feminist take on a feminine-coded genre that's often dismissed out of hand: self-help books. Now we all get to enjoy their wisdom, wit, and discernment distilled into this fabulous book-length exploration of what they learned from living by the rules of fifty self-help books. If you too want to be fine, read this book!"

—Kate Manne, author of *Down Girl: The Logic of Misogyny*

"As someone who is both deeply skeptical of the self-help genre and also in need of . . . so much help, this book was perfect for me. Jolenta and Kristen are doing God's work, and I'm an atheist!"   —John Early, comedian

"Greenberg and Meinzer know something about self-help books. . . . The two have dedicated two weeks each to the advice of more than fifty self-help books. . . . They are honest about the lessons they learned as well as the ones they just couldn't fit into their lives. . . . Even newbies to the genre will enjoy their humorous, clear-eyed views."   —*Booklist*

"Greenberg and Meinzer offer up universal foibles with a sense of humor and encourage readers to explore an array of avenues to self-improvement. . . . Funny and wise, this will be particularly helpful to aficionados of the personal growth genre."   —*Library Journal*

HOW TO BE
Fine

Also by Kristen Meinzer

So You Want to Start a Podcast

HOW TO BE

Fine

WHAT WE LEARNED FROM
LIVING BY THE RULES OF

50

SELF-HELP BOOKS

**JOLENTA GREENBERG
AND KRISTEN MEINZER**

wm

WILLIAM MORROW
An Imprint of HarperCollinsPublishers

HarperCollins books may be purchased for educational, business, or sales promotional use. For information, please email the Special Markets Department at SPsales@harpercollins.com.

A hardcover edition of this book was published in 2020 by William Morrow, an imprint of HarperCollins Publishers.

FIRST WILLIAM MORROW PAPERBACK EDITION PUBLISHED 2021.

Designed by Bonni Leon-Berman

Library of Congress Cataloging-in-Publication Data has been applied for.

ISBN 978-0-06-295720-7

21 22 23 24 25 LSC 10 9 8 7 6 5 4 3 2 1

For our listeners and our husbands

I don't like to give advice. I like to give people information because everyone's life is different, and everyone's journey is different.

—DOLLY PARTON

CONTENTS

INTRODUCTION

Kristen

Halfway through day two, I was crying because I ate two pickle slices and a leaf of lettuce. I knew I was cheating, and I felt horrible about myself. According to the rules of the book I was living by, I was supposed to consume only boiled leeks or the water that came off of boiled leeks, and I was failing. This was all happening just a week after I threw out half my earthly possessions and three weeks after I moved traffic with my mind.

I was living by a diet book called *French Women Don't Get Fat*. The week before, I was living by *The Life-Changing Magic of Tidying Up*. Three weeks earlier, I was living by *The Secret*. This was my life. Every two weeks, I lived by a different self-help book, following all the rules down to the letter: eating what the books said to eat; talking as the books said to talk; waking, sleeping, decorating, and interacting with my husband according to each book's doctrine. And I was recording it all for a reality-show podcast called By the Book.

The person who roped me into this life was my brilliant and hilarious friend Jolenta Greenberg. Jolenta is a comedian, storyteller, voice actor, teacher, and self-help enthusiast. She is a woman who loves crystals and talks earnestly about chakras and truly wants to believe the promises that self-help books routinely shill. The reason she asked me to cohost By the Book with her was that my views were exactly the opposite.

I thought it would be good for a laugh. We would have fun. We would be ridiculous. We would make an entertaining show.

Little did I know that all these books would actually change my life—sometimes even for the better. If not for By the Book, I never would have penned that Amish romance novel I'd always joked about writing. I never would have traveled back to my past lives. And I'm not sure I would have had some of the difficult conversations I've had with my husband about our marriage.

By the Book started off as a wacky experiment, but over the course of its life, it's come to be something much bigger—and not just for us. We have a Facebook community of more than fifteen thousand people from around the world who talk with one another every day about topics that range from workplace drama to alcohol abuse. We've headlined live events for the likes of *The New York Times* and given interviews to NPR, the BBC, the CBC, and even RNZ (that's Radio New Zealand). And we've been written up by *The Guardian, The Washington Post, Time, Bust, BuzzFeed,* IndieWire, and the librarians of Lawrence, Kansas.

But despite all our appearances, interviews, episodes, and Facebook community, listeners still want to know more. Why don't you two write a self-help book sharing what you've learned from living by all these books? we're often asked.

And so, we've written this book. Obviously, we hope it satisfies our existing audience. But our dream is that it also speaks to people who've never heard of us—people who just want to know what two very honest women have to say about how their lives have been upended and improved by methodically following the advice of fifty self-help books in three years.

Note: Our goal is not to tell you how to live your lives. In the grand scheme of things, we're not what you would call experts. We're not psychologists or doctors. And we honestly don't believe we know more than you do about how to be the best version of yourself. As Jolenta often says, Only you are an expert in you.

We're really just here to share our story, and to talk about what's worked for us and what hasn't. And for what it's worth, those things don't include mushy missives like "Empower your heart." Yes, mush can be inspiring and fun. But it can also be hard to actually put into practice.

Thus, we'll be talking only about concrete steps we've taken. That means things you can try at home if that's really and truly what you want to do. But if you just want to laugh or shake your head as we recount how we've tortured ourselves in the name of betterment, that's also fine by us.

You do you, and we'll do us.

WHAT YOU SHOULD KNOW ABOUT

Jolenta

When I was a tender, mouth-breathing five-year-old, I started kindergarten. On my first day I brought with me a box of tissues. Each kindergartener was tasked with bringing in a box of tissues on the first day, and the boxes were supposed to live in our cubbies and be at our disposal for all our snot needs throughout the year.

Come pickup time on my first day, my mother and my kindergarten teacher, Mrs. Marshall, watched in confusion as my tiny hands struggled to jam my tissue box back in my little neon pink backpack. I was clearly planning on taking my tissues home while all around me, my classmates were leaving their tissues in their cubbies without giving them a second thought.

"You can leave those in your cubby," Mrs. Marshall explained. "They'll be safe here and waiting for you every day."

Yeah, right, I thought. *I'm not gonna leave my stuff in a strange room all night! Not on my watch!*

I kept packing up and responded with a meek "I'm okay" as I zipped up my bag and indicated I was ready to hit the road by pulling on my mom's coat.

Mrs. Marshall and my mom exchanged amused glances

and through muffled laughter concluded that I'd leave my tissues at school once I felt ready.

This ritual continued every day. Every morning I'd unpack my tissue box, lovingly leaving it in my cubby, and every afternoon I'd pack my tissues up and take them home for the night, while my mom and teacher chuckled and reminded me I was free to leave them at school permanently. When I was ready.

And boom, one day after two weeks it happened. I was ready. I had sussed out the situation, figured out the rules for myself, and decided it was finally time to trust in the system.

This is one of my mom's favorite stories about me, because it perfectly encapsulates my idiosyncrasies. I'm always two weeks behind. I'm always catching up on life. I'm always just a few beats behind all of life's prescribed "normal" milestones, getting to them a bit later than everyone else. Whether it's getting comfortable leaving my tissues at school, having my first kiss, falling in love, getting a "real" job . . . I'm always running behind.

My proclivity for being two weeks behind in life has followed me for the past thirty-odd years, and it's why I became obsessed with self-help. During my teenage years I discovered that tons of people have written all sorts of rule books about how to live! I knew if I could read them all and implement all their rules, I could catch up to everyone else and finally stop worrying about being behind in life.

As an adult I dabbled in self-help, reading the occasional book and watching the occasional inspirational Internet video. But when one of my four part-time jobs landed me in a newsroom at a radio station, things got real. I was in charge of going through all the books sent to the show I worked on, and we got sent *many* self-help books that no one wanted . . . except me. I wanted them all.

Each new self-help book I'd open was a beautifully bound bundle of promises—of happiness, productivity, success, all things I desperately wanted. Each book I opened was basically saying, "Come on, Jolenta, I'll fix you. You don't want to be two weeks behind forever, do you!?!"

No! I did not. So I took all the books, called my friend and coworker Kristen, and told her we were going to start a project for which we'd strictly live by the rules of the different self-help books I'd been collecting.

Kristen is the kind of friend who is so on top of her life that it's infuriating. She's the anti-me. She's the friend you go to when you need advice on all things "adult." Whether you have questions about real estate lawyers or how to deal with estranged family members, Kristen has your answer. She doesn't need fixing, like me, and that's why I knew she'd be my perfect self-help partner. She'd keep me accountable and serve as a sort of control group, since she was the one who wasn't perpetually trying to catch up. If the books could enhance both of our lives, they worked for real.

And that's how our podcast, By the Book, was born. Timing, work friendships, and a lifetime of being two weeks behind all came together to create an experiment in living by the rules of self-help books for (you guessed it) two weeks at a time.

THE THING ABOUT

Kristen

Jolenta sometimes refers to me as the last person on earth who needs self-help books. I am, for the most part, a happy person. I don't spend a lot of time being anxious or thinking I'm a loser. I have resting jolly face.

On top of that, Jolenta thinks I'm good at adulting. I've been working full-time since high school and paid my own way through college. I have a 401(k), an accountant, and a real estate attorney. I go to the doctor when I need to and I buy toilet paper before I run out.

This isn't to say I'm a perfect specimen of what a human can or should be. Far from it. I always have large piles of paper laying around and I rarely clean or cook for myself. My beloved husband, Dean, does those things. Like most Americans I could probably stand for less screen time and fewer Cheetos. Even though it might be good for me, I don't look at myself in the mirror every single day and exclaim, "What a gorgeous lady!"

And I've had my fair share of problems over the years. I went to seven schools growing up, many of which counted me as the only nonwhite person in my class. I was abused by my father and stepmother so seriously that they lost their rights to see me when I was twelve. I battled disordered eating beginning in grade school and well into my twenties. In college, I dated more than one guy who called me names, stole my money, or wouldn't be seen in public with me. I've been sexually harassed by bosses. And I held both my mother and grandmother in my arms as they died.

Despite all this, I know I'm lucky. A lot of people go through all I have and much, much worse, but without good friends. Plenty of people have brains that are wired to process trauma in a, well, more traumatic way than my brain does. Lots of folks have bodies that don't work the way they want them to, while I do. And far too many people don't feel empowered to—or can't afford to—seek help from mental health professionals (I've seen plenty over the years).

But the truth is, I still get down sometimes. I think this is natural. I think our lives are filled with ebbs and flows. Sometimes we wake up feeling fabulous. Sometimes, later that same day, we feel ornery. Sometimes there's something deep inside of us that doesn't feel quite satisfied.

I'm guessing that's why there are so many self-help books in the world. If people felt content all the time, there wouldn't be any need for them.

That being said, I've always looked upon self-help books with suspicion. A lot of them seem to prey on people's insecurities, and the covers often make promises that are impossible for any one volume to deliver on ("The one guaranteed way to change your life!" "The number one way to make more money in the next year!" "The only proven method for getting your child to sleep!").

Of course, this is why Jolenta and I make such a good team. For all the hope she brings to self-help books, I bring a dose of skepticism. For every promise she wants to believe, there's a promise I want to shoot holes in.

Also, I have a background as a critic. All through college I was an arts and entertainment critic. For years, I worked in a university office where the main purpose was to deconstruct media. And shortly before cocreating By the Book, I wrapped a six-year gig cohosting a film review podcast.

But to be clear, I don't just play the role of a critic when Jolenta and I live by self-help books. Hardly. At this point in the game, I think it's safe to say that I've cried just as much as she has on the show, if not more. I've shared way more than I initially wanted to. And I've willingly opened my personal life up to loads of criticism.

And did I mention that I've learned a thing or two? In some cases, I've just had my suspicions confirmed. In others, I've actually felt my life improve. Some of this improvement stems from my friendship with Jolenta growing and evolving through our show. I'm incredibly grateful for her. Some of this improvement comes from sharing my stories with people who may truly benefit from them. And some of it—yes, I'll admit—comes from living by these ridiculous books.

All right. Enough of my backstory. Let's get to how these books have enhanced and destroyed my life, and Jolenta's.

THE FULL LIST
OF BOOKS
WE'VE LIVED BY,
IN ORDER, SO FAR

- *The Secret* by Rhonda Byrne
- *The Life-Changing Magic of Tidying Up: The Japanese Art of Decluttering and Organizing* by Marie Kondo
- *French Women Don't Get Fat: The Secret of Eating for Pleasure* by Mireille Guiliano
- *The Memory Book: The Classic Guide to Improving Your Memory at Work, at School, and at Play* by Harry Lorayne and Jerry Lucas
- *Past Lives, Future Healing: A Psychic Reveals the Secrets to Good Health and Great Relationships* by Sylvia Browne
- *America's Cheapest Family Gets You Right on the Money: Your Guide to Living Better, Spending Less, and Cashing in on Your Dreams* by Steve Economides and Annette Economides
- *Men Are from Mars, Women Are from Venus: The Classic Guide to Understanding the Opposite Sex* by John Gray
- *Class with the Countess: How to Live with Elegance and Flair* by LuAnn de Lesseps
- *How to Write an Ebook in Less Than 7–14 Days That Will Make You Money Forever* by Darren Ackers

- *Bored and Brilliant: How Spacing Out Can Unlock Your Most Productive and Creative Self* by Manoush Zomorodi
- *The Little Book of Hygge: Danish Secrets to Happy Living* by Meik Wiking
- *Why Good Things Happen to Good People: How to Live a Longer, Healthier, Happier Life by the Simple Act of Giving* by Stephen G. Post and Jill Neimark
- *The Miracle Morning: The Not-So-Obvious Secret Guaranteed to Transform Your Life (Before 8AM)* by Hal Elrod
- *What to Say When You Talk to Your Self* by Shad Helmstetter
- *The 5 Love Languages: The Secret to Love That Lasts* by Gary Chapman
- *The Wild Unknown Tarot Deck and Guidebook* by Kim Krans
- *The Subtle Art of Not Giving a F*ck: A Counterintuitive Approach to Living a Good Life* by Mark Manson
- *You Are a Badass: How to Stop Doubting Your Greatness and Start Living an Awesome Life* by Jen Sincero
- *Meditation for Fidgety Skeptics: A 10% Happier How-To Book* by Dan Harris and Jeff Warren, with Carlye Adler
- *Zero Waste Home: The Ultimate Guide to Simplifying Your Life by Reducing Your Waste* by Bea Johnson
- *Presence: Bringing Your Boldest Self to Your Biggest Challenges* by Amy Cuddy

- *The Nature Fix: Why Nature Makes Us Happier, Healthier, and More Creative* by Florence Williams
- *A Girl's Guide to Joining the Resistance: A Feminist Handbook on Fighting for Good* by Emma Gray
- *The 4-Hour Workweek: Escape 9–5, Live Anywhere, and Join the New Rich* by Timothy Ferriss
- *The Curated Closet: A Simple System for Discovering Your Personal Style and Building Your Dream Wardrobe* by Anuschka Rees
- "How to Apologize" by the Greater Good Science Center at UC Berkeley
- *Girl, Wash Your Face: Stop Believing the Lies About Who You Are So You Can Become Who You Were Meant to Be* by Rachel Hollis
- *A Simple Act of Gratitude: How Learning to Say Thank You Changed My Life* by John Kralik
- *Year of Yes: How to Dance It Out, Stand in the Sun and Be Your Own Person* by Shonda Rhimes
- *Pick Three: You Can Have It All (Just Not Every Day)* by Randi Zuckerberg
- *Pantsdrunk (Kalsarikänni): The Finnish Path to Relaxation* by Miska Rantanen
- *Big Magic: Creative Living Beyond Fear* by Elizabeth Gilbert
- *Astrology for Happiness and Success: From Aries to Pisces, Create the Life You Want—Based on Your Astrological Sign!* by Mecca Woods

- *The Four Agreements: A Practical Guide to Personal Freedom* by Don Miguel Ruiz
- *The 9 Steps to Financial Freedom: Practical and Spiritual Steps So You Can Stop Worrying* by Suze Orman
- *The Body Is Not an Apology: The Power of Radical Self-Love* by Sonya Renee Taylor
- *How to Hold a Grudge: From Resentment to Contentment—the Power of Grudges to Transform Your Life* by Sophie Hannah
- *The Sleep Revolution: Transforming Your Life, One Night at a Time* by Arianna Huffington
- *Getting Things Done: The Art of Stress-Free Productivity* by David Allen
- *Next Level Basic: The Definitive Basic Bitch Handbook* by Stassi Schroeder
- *The Art of Dying Well: A Practical Guide to a Good End of Life* by Katy Butler
- *So You Want to Start a Podcast: Finding Your Voice, Telling Your Story, and Building a Community That Will Listen* by Kristen Meinzer
- *How to Win Friends and Influence People* by Dale Carnegie
- *On Being a Real Person* by Harry Emerson Fosdick
- *The Power of Positive Thinking* by Norman Vincent Peale
- *Phyllis Diller's Housekeeping Hints* by Phyllis Diller
- *The Joy of Sex: A Gourmet Guide to Love Making* by Alex Comfort

- *The Dance of Anger: A Woman's Guide to Changing the Patterns of Intimate Relationships* by Harriet Lerner
- *Who Moved My Cheese?: An A-Mazing Way to Deal with Change in Your Work and in Your Life* by Spencer Johnson
- *The Gifts of Imperfection: Let Go of Who You Think You're Supposed to Be and Embrace Who You Are* by Brené Brown

PART 1

13

Things That Worked

COMMIT ACTS
OF KINDNESS

Kristen

Friends, I feel it would be totally disingenuous if I didn't come right out and admit it: I love being nice. I love giving compliments to friends and strangers. I adore starting off each day by yelling a jolly good morning to an office full of coworkers. Giving up my seat on the subway for a person who might need it is one of my favorite things. Being nice is the best!

And so, it should come as no surprise that it was my idea to live by *Why Good Things Happen to Good People,* a ten-step guide to kindness and happiness, by Jill Neimark and Stephen G. Post.

Full disclosure: Jolenta hated this book. She found it cheesy, occasionally dated, and narrow in its scope. And yes, I'll agree that the book has its faults.

That being said, when we lived by it, even Jolenta admitted that it gave her a taste of "what it must feel like to be one of the happy people." And it's not the only book to do this. *A Girl's Guide to Joining the Resistance* by Emma Gray and

Zero Waste Home by Bea Johnson are just two more that did the same thing.

In fact, every time we've lived by a book that encourages us to commit acts of kindness and altruism, we've both felt better. And not just because being a goody two-shoes gives us an excuse to feel self-righteous about being better citizens or wins us the admiration of strangers. Kindness just feels good.

We've seen this with the people in our immediate lives— our husbands, our friends, our coworkers. For example, while we were living by *Good Things,* I was promoted to a managerial position. I thought about all the times new managers had come into my life over the years and taken over without checking in with the existing staff and asking what they needed. I wanted to do things differently. And so I embarked on my new position by having one-on-one meetings with every person on my team. I asked what issues they felt needed the most attention, where they felt unsupported, and what they liked and didn't like about how things currently stood.

Of course, I wasn't able to fix all the things that needed fixing in my department. But this listening tour made me feel more connected with my team.

For both Jolenta and me, kindness also created a greater sense of connection with people we didn't know. For example, in looking for people to help in her day-to-day life, Jolenta noticed all the women carrying their strollers—with their babies still in them—up and down the often treacherous New York City subway stairs. And every chance she got, she helped them. She put herself in the shoes of those mothers and did a tiny bit of labor for them. Those little acts of kindness made it impossible for her not to feel more connected with her fellow humans.

This isn't to say that Jolenta had never noticed these women before, or offered to help them. She had. But it wasn't something she deliberately set out to do each day, and when she did, she felt happier.

To our tremendous relief, we also found that doing the right thing helped empower us in the face of past traumas. Specifically, Jolenta and I both decided while living by *Why Good Things Happen to Good People* to speak up about how we'd been mistreated by men in power. She spoke up by performing a stand-up set pillorying a former boss who'd hit on her. I spoke up by reaching out to the president of my prior workplace, reporting the host of a show who had sexually harassed me.

Coincidentally, not long after we spoke up, an investigative reporter named Suki Kim reached out to both of us, asking us to share our stories. She had a much larger platform than either of us did, which meant our acts of decency, kindness, bravery, or whatever you want to call them would help more people than either of us could on our own. Her story made international headlines and became one of the pivotal writings on the #MeToo movement in 2017.

But whether our actions attract international headlines or no attention at all, we know we're making ourselves feel happier when we're kind. For example, when I feel down, helping strangers carry their groceries or shovel their cars out of snow piles elevates my spirits. When I'm not feeling great about myself, complimenting friends and strangers gives my mood a boost (fun fact: I've found this also works when I deliver the compliments behind people's backs—or positively gossip, as some people call it). And when we're feeling misunderstood, trying our best, with kindness and humor, to build bridges—as Jolenta attempted with her mother-in-law while living by one book—can make our hearts feel lighter (and our relationships less strained).

For me, there's probably no greater wellness practice than waking up each day and thinking, *What can I do to make someone else's life a little better today?* and then making sure, through my words and actions, to turn that one person into two or five or ten. Invariably, one of the people whose day is most improved will be me.

And I can't say it enough: Being kind is fun. Just observe a group of small children playing, taking turns being banker, pushing each other on swings, and playing fair. Looking at them and their joy, who wouldn't prefer to be kind? It's way more fun than being mean.

ENGAGE IN POSITIVE SELF-TALK

Jolenta

I've said it before and I'll say it again: When you have social anxiety, you eat and drink a lot of things you don't want to consume. The thought of possibly offending someone or being rejected is so nerve-racking that rather than sending food back or saying you don't like something, you suck it up and pretend everything is fine. So if I'm at my in-laws' and allergic to the main dish at dinner, I'll try to secretly load up on sides while strategically putting bits of the food I can't eat onto my husband's plate so it looks like I'm all good. Or if I'm at a bar and order a margarita but get served a gin and tonic, I'll drink that gin even though I don't like it (sorry, gin lovers, I had a bad experience with it back in the day).

Why do I do this? I have social anxiety, which means my mind is plagued by a constantly rotating carousel of thoughts, worries, and heightened fears about how others are perceiving me. So I might think things like *If my in-laws see me not eating, they'll think I'm a rude, spoiled bitch, and they won't love me anymore, and then they'll tell my husband not to love me.* Or I'll have this thought running through my brain: *Don't send this drink back; the bartender doesn't care if you hate gin. Don't make this her problem; she's super-busy tonight and if you add your complaint to her life you're making her job harder and basically not supporting women!*

This extreme fear of social rejection means I end up eating and drinking things I don't want or don't like *all the time*. It's embarrassing but true.

I'm used to carrying around this fear of social situations and the tape of self-deprecating thoughts that runs through my head to scold me into avoiding any kind of rejection. I've had this tape my whole life (hence my calling it a tape—cuz I was born in the eighties, when we actually used tapes!); it's kind of like having a really mean friend in your brain at all times. A friend who says things like this: *You're a mess. She thinks you're an idiot. You're not doing enough. He thinks you're ugly. You're gonna show up to this party at the wrong time. You're too much for most people. You're a bad friend* and so on. I thought this harsh inner monologue was an immutable part of me, but a book called *What to Say When You Talk to Your Self* by Shad Helmstetter says it's possible to retrain that mean-friend voice to start saying some nicer things.

According to the book (which we lived by during season two of By the Book), this kind of inner berating is called negative self-talk. And self-talk gets more negative over time because from the moment we're born, we're bombarded with messages about what we can and can't do. These messages come from every direction—from our parents, peers, teachers, social media, television, and society at large. We absorb these messages and use them to create the story of who we are.

As we go through life we collect the observations, values, and judgments of others. We take these stances on as though they are reality—because we're little babes simply trying to figure out the ways of the world and don't know any better! Each outside opinion we take on as truth is like a pair of tinted glasses we glue to our faces. Over time we put on all sorts of colored glasses, each one tinted with a different rule about life. One tint tells you who is smart and who is dumb, another tells you what your body should look like, another tint constantly reminds you to say sorry for taking up as much space as the dude next to you . . . The list goes on and on.

We take on so many of these beliefs that we end up walking around with hundreds of pairs of tinted glasses glued to our sweet, shining faces, and all the colors meld into dark, impenetrable blinders. We lose sight of ourselves and instead see a list of inadequacies that we're always aiming to fix. This is negative self-talk.

Here is some of the negative self-talk I often say:

- Your body is repulsive; a man will never be attracted to you and you need a man's approval to succeed in the world.
- You're too negative.
- Curly brown hair is not pretty.

- Your features are too "Jewish."
- You're too tall to find love because guys want to be with only dainty, mousy, superfeminine women.
- Your emotions are too big, you're irrational, and people see you as annoying and crazy.
- You suck at math.

I often think of these things as facts, but they're really just someone else's biased opinions, not immutable truths. In fact, I can list every person I heard these annoying opinions from. See?

- *Your body is repulsive; a man will never be attracted to you and you need a man's approval to succeed in the world* (my ass-hat high school health and PE teacher)
- *You're too negative* (my husband, back when we first started dating)
- *Curly brown hair is not pretty* (the third-grade recess attendant who commented one day that my friend with straight blond hair was the "most adorable")
- *Your features are too "Jewish"* (the non-Jewish side of my family)
- *You're too tall to find love because guys want to be with only dainty, mousy, superfeminine women* (the dude I was boning when I first moved to New York, who said he was a feminist philosopher but wanted to seriously date only women who never challenged anything he said)

- *Your emotions are too big, you're irrational, and people see you as annoying and crazy* (my mom, because she said the same things about herself when she had emotional reactions)
- *You suck at math* (whoever decided that I randomly belonged in the lower-level math class when I started middle school; side note: Most of the girls in my grade were put in that level without our parents being told)

From living by *What to Say When You Talk to Your Self*, I learned that we hear negative messages (stop kicking that, don't raise your voice, you can't go in there, and so on) more often than positive ones, and they tend to be more specific, too. And a lot of the time we need those messages. I probably wouldn't be alive if I hadn't been taught "Never touch that electrical socket!" or "Stop flipping the bird every time a driver cuts you off!" So I'm very glad these restrictive messages have stuck in my head and kept me safe.

There's a problem with this system of message storage, though. Not all negative messages save our lives. Some are just dumb opinions and don't need to be stored as rules in our little baby brains, but they get stored away nonetheless. So things like "Your hair is too curly to be considered pretty" or "Boys can't play with pink things like that" end up holding the same weight as their life-prolonging counterparts.

As I've grown and matured, I've collected, filed, and set in stone many of these admonishing rules. They run my life at this point. They keep me on time, they keep me from walking into traffic, they even remind me to pee after sex so I don't get a UTI. But they also torture me with stupid rules based on shame, bias, or misinformation. Things like, oh, you know, I guess everything listed a few paragraphs earlier. These internal scolding messages feel like rules I have to live by that make my life harder, but they aren't rules. They're just things I say to myself that I heard from unreliable sources.

So how do we get our self-talk to be kinder? How do we sort through all the rules we've learned about life, weed out the unhelpful ones, and start taking on kind tints that complement one another and together make a rosier outlook, so we can enjoy life more?

Helmstetter says that it's possible to reprogram our thought patterns and undo all that negative self-talk with some new, positive messages. When we lived by *What to Say When You Talk to Your Self,* Kristen and I tried many ways to reprogram our thoughts to be more positive.

This was pretty easy for Kristen. She already consciously tries to say nice things to herself. But you should know this wasn't always the case; it took her years to become as good at this as she is. Not unlike many girls growing up, she spent years feeling horrible about her body and putting herself down, both out loud and in her head. But over time and with lots of work, she slowly started accepting compliments, saying nice things about herself, and eventually believing all these kind words.

I, on the other hand, had never given much thought to what I say to myself until we lived by this book. But after I had tracked how I talk to myself for a day, it became clear I had a self-talk problem. Over the course of twenty-four hours I didn't say one positive thing about myself or to myself. This was heartbreaking; I would never hang out with someone who talked to me the way I talk to me, and I became determined to change this.

So I dove headfirst into the book's different self-talk exercises. Over two weeks I had kind conversations out loud with myself in the shower, wrote kind mantras over and over in a journal, and listened to affirmation podcasts—and the whole time it felt incredibly stupid to have conversations with myself while I washed my hair, and getting caught by my partner listening to recorded affirmations while I was cooking was profoundly embarrassing. Every time I said something complimentary to myself or about myself I felt like a ridiculous fraud who dealt in lies and counterfeit.

At the end of living by *What to Say When You Talk to Your Self,* I wasn't sure I was doing it right. Forcing positive self-talk wasn't feeling natural, and I worried that maybe I was too broken or anxious for the book's advice to work. But then something surprising happened. The night we finished living by that book, I was served a very flat glass of prosecco while at a bar in Brooklyn celebrating a friend's birthday. Since prosecco is my go-to drink and my overblown fear of social ridicule means I never send anything back, I drink my fair share of flat prosecco. But that night, without even thinking twice, I just strutted up to the bar and with a self-assuredness I didn't know I had, I asked the bartender for another glass, this time with bubbles.

Whether I felt it working or not, I'm convinced my two weeks of forced positive self-talk helped me do something with confidence that my social anxiety would normally prohibit me from doing. So I consider that a damn good (and bubbly) start.

Dear Kristen and Jolenta,

I've tried practicing positive self-talk, but every time I do, I feel like a liar. What's the point in saying nice things to myself if I don't believe what I'm saying?

—SH

Dear SH,

Believe us—we feel your pain. As Jolenta was just saying, she didn't use to believe the sunny affirmations she said to herself either. She still struggles to. And yet, positive self-talk still seemed to make a difference in her life. Before living by *What to Say When You Talk to Your Self,* she felt unable to speak up when she was served flat prosecco. After, she did.

The point here: Maybe she didn't have to consciously believe all the nice things she said to herself for those nice things to make a difference. Maybe she just had to let them wash over her like the sounds of advertisements on TV, songs on the radio, and all the other noises in the modern world that tell us what we should think about ourselves, even if we're not consciously listening.

For me, the path to being kinder to myself was driven by my desire to be kinder to others. As is the case with a lot of girls in America, my childhood habit when complimented on my appearance was to reply with "No, my skin looks horrible" or "I can barely fit into this dress, I'm sure I look like a sausage."

At one point, someone I admired said to me, "Will you please just say 'Thank you' when people compliment you? Every time you deny their compliments you're essentially saying they're idiots with no power of observation." Another person I admired put it more bluntly: "You sound like you're fishing for more compliments every time you deny someone's kind words."

I was mortified. Was I really coming off as such a jerk? I didn't mean to be. I was just trying to be honest. I really and truly believed I looked like a monster most of the time.

But driven by my desire to be kinder to others, I began to accept compliments more graciously. Over time, that led to me internalizing what some of those complimentary words were saying. And it also led me to a realization: I never complimented myself. I talked to myself like I was the worst, ugliest, most unworthy person on the planet. I talked to myself as I would never talk to anyone else. And thank god for therapy and good friends for helping me to realize I could do better.

My point: Accepting compliments also felt like a lie to me in the beginning. But I did it to be kind to others. And that kindness to others eventually led to me being kinder to myself. I worked with the lie, until it became the truth. And now I know what the real lie was.

—Kristen

PRACTICE GRATITUDE

Kristen

At least 10 percent of the books Jolenta and I have lived by have told us to practice gratitude, but the ways of and reasons for doing so have varied wildly.

For example, when we were living by *The Secret,* by Rhonda Byrne, gratitude was just one of many small steps we were advised to take in order to get what we wanted out of life (along with making vision boards, imagining our futures, and just outright telling the universe what we wanted). It was more or less a way of saying, "I'm the kind of person who appreciates what I have, so I should be given more." Personally, I found this version of thanks mercenary and icky.

Other books treat gratitude quite differently. For example, when we were living by Marie Kondo's *The Life-Changing Magic of Tidying Up,* we were told to thank each item we owned for its service. In some cases, we thanked an item that was cluttering our home and that we no longer felt a connection to or needed. We'd say, "Physics textbook, thank you for helping me get through the final semester of college, but it's time you go to someone who can use you again." Alternatively, if something was an impulse buy that we never once used, we'd say, "Thank you, unicorn minidress, for the thrill of buying you. I enjoyed that jolt of energy when I first laid eyes on you, but it's time you go to someone who will actually wear you."

In addition to thanking items we discard, *The Life-Changing Magic of Tidying Up* recommends thanking items we keep. For example, the book suggests emptying out your handbag at the end of the day so that it can rest, and thanking the bag for its service. I didn't enjoy emptying out my bag; doing so led to wasting extra time every evening and morning on what I considered an unnecessary task. But I did enjoy thanking my bag, as well as my clothes and bed and apartment and all the other objects that help me live the life I want. I loved coming home from work, kicking off my shoes, and saying, "Thank you, shoes, for helping me to walk around this city I love." I loved taking off my glasses at night and saying, "Thank you for helping me to see the beauty in the world a bit more clearly."

But my very favorite approach to gratitude was in a book by John Kralik called *A Simple Act of Gratitude*. In a single year, Kralik set out to write 365 thank-you notes. Initially, he did it as a way to feel less hopeless. When he embarked on his project, he wasn't sure his life was worth living. But with each letter he wrote and tracked, he was able to literally count his blessings. At the same time, the act of sitting down each day with pen and paper helped to retrain his brain to focus more on the good things in life and less on the bad.

But Kralik didn't just write letters. He also made a practice of answering simple how-are-yous with things he was grateful for rather than complaints. When he was feeling down, he would play the Glad Game, which he first learned about while reading Eleanor H. Porter's classic children's book *Pollyanna* to his daughter. In the Glad Game, players list all the things they're happy about—not as a way of denying their pain, but as a way to muster the fortitude to get through life's challenges.

I absolutely adored living by Kralik's book. At the time we lived by it, the branch of the company I was working for had just decided to fold. I was worried about my direct reports and concerned for myself. And on top of that, I had medical issues that required surgery. I was feeling down.

But writing thank-you letters helped me to feel a bit better. I wrote a note to each person on my team who was let go, thanking them for all their hard work and for making my life happier. I wrote to my doctors, thanking them for their care and support. And I even wrote a letter to the boss who made the final decision to close my department, thanking him for all the opportunities he gave me over the years.

These letters allowed me to focus on how fortunate I was—not just for good medical care and good opportunities, but for all the people in my life whom I was lucky enough to know and feel supported by. How much more horrible would my life be had I been forced to face all my troubles alone? Writing thank-you notes reminded me I wasn't alone, and I probably never would be.

And I have to also point out that practicing gratitude is fun. It is so much more joyful than looking at all the ways life is imperfect, or envying others who have more. It is a true joy to admire birds and be thankful we live in a world where animals can fly. It is a pleasure to tell my husband I appreciate all he does for me and feel the gratitude in my bones. And yes, to go back to Marie Kondo, the world feels a little more magical when I thank my shoes and glasses for all they do for me.

Now, before I wrap this up, I feel it's only right for me to mention Jolenta's experience with gratitude here. While Jolenta had fun with gratitude living by *The Secret* and still sings the praises of *The Life-Changing Magic of Tidying Up,* she had mixed feelings about Kralik's book. Focusing on thanks every day reminded her of all she should be thankful for, but it also reminded her of the fact that she took a lot of things in her life for granted. Combined, those feelings made her wonder, *What's wrong with me? Why can't I just be thankful for what I have? This book makes me feel like a jerk.*

And a bigger criticism she had of Kralik's book was that it didn't focus more on giving back. As Jolenta sees it, thanking means you're receiving. But if you're receiving, shouldn't you also be giving? And while, yes, Kralik raised thousands of dollars for charity and helped his direct reports and family by the end of his experiment, it's true that he didn't necessarily instruct his readers to do the same.

All that being said, Jolenta will grudgingly admit that living by *A Simple Act of Gratitude* made her happier. Thanks to the book, she reached out to people like her grandmother, to whom she hadn't talked in a while, and thanked them for being in her life. Those moments of thanks led to bigger conversations and feelings of connection. And when Jolenta and her husband, Brad, played the Glad Game, the shift from frustration to humor to tenderness between the two of them was palpable.

In short, even a gratitude skeptic like Jolenta felt her life improved with a bit of thanks. And for a gratitude lover like me, being thankful each day made truly tough times more bearable. And for that, I'm thankful.

Dear Kristen and Jolenta,

You've demonstrated on your show and in other public arenas that you're both activists. How can you be so grateful and be activists at the same time? Doesn't one negate the other? Doesn't a relentless focus on gratitude mean you're turning a blind eye to climate change and racism and all the other issues you're actively trying to fight? There's so much *not* to be grateful for!

—NG

Dear NG,

I honestly don't believe that being thankful makes me blind to the world's ugliness. Rather, I think it reminds me of what I'm fighting for. Those birds in the sky that I'm so thankful for? They're part of what I want to save. The access I have to outstanding healthcare and a decent education? I don't just self-ishly appreciate them; I also want to fight for every-one else—regardless of race, economic background, gender, or sexual orientation—to have the same access I do.

Also, gratitude gives me a break from despair. If all I did every minute of every day was lament the nega-tive things in the world, I suspect I'd eventually stop getting out of bed. What fighting could I do then?

And gratitude helps to sustain relationships—not just with those we already know and love, but with others who are trying to fight the good fight. We can't be in this alone. Telling people we value them and their contributions is the least we can do.

Yes, I can be thankful, and I can be an activist. In fact, I can't see a way to do one without the other.

—Kristen

TREAT PEOPLE AS THEY WANT TO BE TREATED, NOT AS YOU WANT TO BE TREATED

Jolenta

When I was only a few months into dating the dude I'd end up marrying, we had a fight that perplexed me to no end. Brad, that's his name, took me to brunch at a little place in his neighborhood. The food was great, the vibe was adorable, and I had a lovely meal. To show how much I was enjoying myself I inhaled a plate of huevos rancheros, picked up the bill, and held his hand on the walk home.

However, while we were walking back to his apartment he had a meltdown.

"Why didn't you like brunch?" he whined.

"I loved brunch. What are you talking about?" I shot back.

"You weren't excited enough," he replied, as he let go of my hand and huffily crossed his arms over his chest.

This hurt my feelings. What in the world was he talking about? I wasn't excited enough? What did he want from me? Did he want me to jump up and down and be all girlie about my big hero who'd found the perfect brunch spot? Did he want a medal? Did he want me to bow down to the patriarchy and be a completely different person who fawned over men who could pick restaurants? *No thank you!*

"You're crazy, dude. I don't know what you want from me. I liked my eggs, but I'm not gonna throw you a parade about it" was my friendly reply.

This last comment shut down the argument and we finished our walk back to his place in silence. We got over this argument quickly, distracted by a movie his roommate was watching or something like that. But every once in a while I'd think back to our little brunch exchange with outrage and wonder, *What the hell was that about?*

Fast-forward a few years to the second season of By the Book, when Kristen and I lived by a book that finally shed some light on the Great Brunch Meltdown of 2011.

That book was *The 5 Love Languages,* by Gary Chapman. In it Chapman lays out his theory that there are five ways to express and experience love. These ways, or "love languages," are receiving of gifts, quality time, words of affirmation, acts of service, and physical touch. Chapman believes all people have a primary and a secondary love language that are the easiest ways for them to experience love. Someone who likes touch might rub your feet to say I love you, someone who loves acts of service might feel loved when you empty the dishwasher, and so on. Once you understand a person's love language, you can more easily make them feel loved. Feeling loved leads to better communication and overall happier relationships.

As Kristen and I read that book, it became clear to me that Brad and I have total opposite love languages. His are quality time and words of affirmation. Mine are acts of service and physical touch. When I finished reading, that memory of brunch popped into my head. And it dawned on me then that we were each trying to express and receive love in a language the other didn't understand. I was trying to show him my appreciation through service by picking up the bill and physical touch by holding hands. But, since he doesn't speak those languages, my messages of love and gratitude were missed by him. He wanted me to express my feelings with words, in a love language he spoke fluently.

When we lived by *The 5 Love Languages*, Kristen and I learned way more about our spouses than we ever expected. She began to see that Dean's overly handsy nature was his way of trying to show he loved her, and she was able to tell him she didn't share that language but would work harder to show her affection through physical touch—which she did beautifully when she pushed him by his tushy up the stairs while he carried heavy boxes into their new apartment. And Dean took fewer liberties with his hands and found ways to better speak love languages that Kristen understands, like acts of service (as illustrated through the just mentioned box carrying).

I, on the other hand, learned that I hardly ever compliment my partner. I tease him, and make him the butt of my jokes, and assume because I do chores and give great cuddles he must feel loved by me. I was wrong. When we were living by the book he admitted to me that when I tease him a ton sometimes he truly wonders if I hate him.

This was a wake-up call. I thought I was great at communicating my love to Brad. But because I wasn't speaking his language, my declarations of devotion masked as kisses and my acts of service emptying the dishwasher weren't being received. He saw me pushing myself to try new things and working hard to use nice words and he really felt loved. I think it helped us both get over our own insecurities and put our focus and efforts on each other.

OFFER GRACIOUS
APOLOGIES

Jolenta

In 2016 my husband, Brad, lived on the road reporting on the election all over the country. We were newlyweds and right when we said "I do" to each other he also said "I do" to a fancy new reporting job. He spent our entire first year of marriage going to events with Hillary and Trump, and I spent our first year of marriage working at home being pretty lonely. But all of that was going to change once we went to Argentina after the election.

This was our big plan. We were going to reconnect while trekking through the wilds of Patagonia. While this may sound amazing to most of you, I'm gonna be honest, I am not a fan of trekking. I know I am lucky to have trekked enough to even know the fact that trekking isn't my favorite activity. I spent all my school years at a small school in Oregon that forced yearly backpacking, camping, and hiking treks starting at age ten, and I always associate trips like this with feeling like a kid being forced to do arbitrary activities against her will. Not a fan.

Brad, on the other hand, is a huge fan of treks, adventures, wandering aimlessly . . . all of those cool traveley things. I love his curious, adventurous heart; I love it so much I don't want to disappoint—so that's how I ended up lying to myself and him and agreeing that hiking across an iceberg, and up many windswept cliffs in the pouring rain, was a great way to come together with my beloved after a year apart.

I basically ignored all the planning he was doing. I didn't want to know specifics about which activities I'd be dreading the most, so I simply pretended it wasn't really happening. But while we were on our flight, I figured it was time to face the music and I finally asked about our itinerary in detail. I did not like what I heard.

As Brad listed remote daylong hikes, insane weather, and the fact that we'd have to do this all with strangers in small groups (note: My least favorite thing next to trekking is being forced to do said trekking with small groups of strangers), I ended up having a huge meltdown. I cried for hours as we flew, feeling trapped between wanting to spend time with him and not actually wanting to go on an adventure. While I cried I said mean things to Brad about how he ignores my needs, is selfish, is pushy, and doesn't appreciate me for who I am. These things were all kind of true, to be honest. We had really disconnected while he was away, but screaming this all at him while trapped in an airplane long after having agreed to go along with him on this trip was not helping my case, nor was it very nice.

He apologized a lot for his part. We spent long nights

staying up late talking. We talked all about how I felt our trip was a chance for intimacy that we were wasting on his outdoor adventure fantasies. He asked me all about how I'd felt overlooked during the year he spent away and overlooked as he planned activity after activity he knew I wouldn't want to do. He apologized for not considering my needs without being told; he admitted he knew he was planning things I wouldn't like and resented that I wasn't speaking up, so he kept planning more and more. *He* apologized, asked how he could make things up to me, and he started taking action right away. That night he changed our itinerary for me, so we'd spend more time in the city. And when we got back home he found a couples therapist for us to start seeing so we could work together on our communication and he could work on showing his empathy for me.

I can tell you, almost three years later, all of this work is paying off. We've never again gotten to a place as low as we were on that flight (which is funny because you'd think that you couldn't be hitting rock bottom in your marriage while flying in the air). But there was one thing wrong with how we moved forward. I never really dealt with my part . . .

That's right, I never apologized to Brad for berating him for hours, telling him he was inconsiderate, selfish, and incapable of thinking of me and my needs. I threatened divorce on that flight and called him many mean names, and I got away with it.

From then on anytime we had to travel Brad and I would fight. Planning trips and holiday visits was a nightmare. I just figured we were bad at traveling and would be for the rest of our lives. But then Kristen and I were asked by The Science of Happiness podcast to be their happiness guinea pigs and learn how to give an effective apology.

The Science of Happiness is a show that brings together science and stories about living a meaningful life. Based out of UC Berkeley and produced in tandem with the university's Greater Good Science Center, the show highlights the most provocative and practical scientific findings about compassion, gratitude, mindfulness, and awe.

Kristen and I were asked to follow the guidelines laid out by the center on how to give a truly effective apology. After getting our assignment, I sat down with Brad and asked him if there was anything in our ten-year history that he felt was unresolved and could maybe use an apology.

I assumed he wouldn't come up with anything and would tell me I was such a perfect wife there was no way in hell he'd feel like there were any unresolved issues between us. I was wrong. It took him only a split second to say, "I mean there's the way you handled Argentina. You said a lot of hurtful things on that flight and I did a lot of work to learn from the mistakes I made back then, but you never really did."

Oh no! He was right. He totally deserved an apology for how I acted. So I got to work using my new guidelines to craft the perfect "sorry about Argentina" speech. You'd think this would be a monumental undertaking. But it was surprisingly simple.

All I had to do to make amends was acknowledge what I did wrong, explain the misguided intentions behind what

I did, share my remorse by communicating what I regret doing and how I'll work to not do that in the future, and last, offer a way to repair the damage done.

I followed the rules and apologized to Brad for misleading him by acting okay with everything until it was too late because I was afraid to disappoint him. I told him I could easily see how he must have felt like I lied to him by acting as if everything was fine until it was way too late. I promised to do better voicing my preferences in the future and offered to help plan our next trip so we wouldn't end up in the same predicament.

When I finished telling Brad all these things, it was like I had put a magic spell on him. He was over-the-moon happy because he finally felt understood and reassured. And it didn't just end there. I followed through on my offer to be more involved in our travel, and we just went on a trip to Jamaica that was awesome for both of us—and no one had a meltdown on the flight.

And what's great about apologies is you can make them no matter how big or small the issue is. They work with big hot-button issues and little everyday accidents. Kristen's Happiness Guinea Pig apology is the perfect example of this. (Is it me, or is Kristen the perfect example of most things?)

Kristen's apology was to her husband, Dean, for accidentally breaking his favorite kitchen tool. She used her effective apology to acknowledge how she'd be more careful in the future and offered to buy Dean a replacement.

From little mistakes to divorce-threatening blowouts,

being acknowledged and reassured helps alleviate the pain of those we hurt. And if we learned anything from *Why Good Things Happen to Good People,* it is that putting positivity into the world and righting any wrongs we've left unresolved can only bring about more positive things in the future. Or at least better vacations and unbroken kitchen gadgets.

Dear Kristen and Jolenta,

Women are brought up to apologize all the time for everything. We're supposed to apologize when someone bumps into us. We're supposed to apologize when someone misinterprets what we say. We're supposed to apologize from the day we're born until the day we die. Shouldn't you be telling your female audience to apologize less?

—NS

Dear NS,

We're sorry! Ha! Just kidding. We're not sorry. But we do understand where you're coming from. And we absolutely agree with you to a point. Yes, women are told to apologize all the time, including moments when we've done nothing wrong (and we understand that many of our Canadian followers of all genders suffer from this same social programming).

But to be clear: We're not asking you to apologize

more. We're actually not asking you to do anything! We just want to illustrate how apologizing in a more targeted way—focused on understanding, remorse, restitution, and a deeper sense of human connection—made us feel better. It also made those we wronged feel better.

That being said, we do wish certain people would practice more effective apologizing. Specifically, we're referring to politicians, captains of industry, and people in power more broadly—many of whom refuse to admit when they've done something wrong, much less try to make things right.

So, NS, if you happen to be one of these people in power, I'm going to backtrack and say: Yes, we actually do want you to apologize more, and apologize more effectively. Doing so will make you a more decent human being and more popular with the masses, regardless of your gender. And isn't that what you want? Of course it is.

—Kristen

GET OFF
YOUR DEVICE

Kristen

I am not what you would call a digital native. I did not grow up with a cellphone or Internet. We didn't have a home computer or even a TV with a remote control. The most sophisticated piece of entertainment technology we had in my house when I was growing up was a dual-cassette deck and record-playing stereo, which I bought in junior high school after saving up months of babysitting money.

This lack of technology is partly because I'm a few years past being a millennial. It's also because my parents had absolutely no interest in gadgets. They didn't see the point of them. When I wanted to use a computer, I went to my aunt Elaine's house. She had an ancient Apple II.

I inherited my parents' lack of interest in technology. When a new gizmo comes out, I usually don't care. Alternatively, I might find myself a bit suspicious and asking a lot of questions. What if this product is just a flash in the pan? (I'm talking to you, PalmPilot.) Or what if there are loads of kinks to work out? (Yes, you, first-generation Apple mouse.) Also, why is this new piece of metal so freaking expensive?

Once I finally decide to purchase a gadget, you'd better believe I use it until it's dead. I will replace the batteries and parts. I will do anything I can to keep my machine going. I don't care if it's out of fashion. You know what I do care about? Depleting the world of more natural resources for the sake of a new gizmo. And throwing yet another device into the landfill. And wasting money. No, thanks. That's why I was the last person in America to buy a cellular flip phone, and why I continued to use that little flip phone until four years ago, when it inevitably stopped working and the Verizon store stopped carrying them, and I was forced to buy a smartphone with a touch screen like the rest of civilization.

And so, I was a bit surprised when Jolenta and I tracked our screen time for Manoush Zomorodi's *Bored and Brilliant* to find that I stare at my smartphone almost as much as she stares at hers.

Jolenta, by her own admission, loves her phone. She's referred to it as her life, her best friend, her everything. She began using a cellphone in high school. Her father liked technology and kept it in the house. And during our time living by *Bored and Brilliant*, she discovered that she looks at her phone for over two hours a day.

When I got real about my technology usage, I also realized my phone was my life, despite my claims of being a Luddite. Turns out, the last thing I do before going to bed each night is look at my phone. The first thing I do each morning is look at my phone. Several evenings a week, I scroll through eBay while watching TV with my husband

and he sits beside me playing video games. I go onto the By the Book Facebook community and Twitter pages at least once an hour to check on the conversations there. What's worse, I lie to myself about why I keep looking—I'll tell myself it's to moderate comment threads or let new people in, but the fact is, I'm addicted.

Of course, I'd convinced myself I wasn't addicted for years—and not just because I grew up in a tech-averse house. I was proud of the facts that I didn't play video games and that I never texted while behind the wheel, even at a stoplight. I smugly watched people texting at restaurants and ignoring their families and thought, *I'll never be like that*. I told myself I wasn't chained to my phone.

But if I was looking at my phone for two hours a day, maybe I was.

Now it's important to note that *Bored and Brilliant* wasn't just about tracking our phone usage. And to be clear, it wasn't really even about cutting down on how often we used our phones (spoiler: At the end of two weeks, Jolenta and I found that we'd cut down our use by only a few minutes). It was about freeing our brains to be—as the title suggests—a little more bored and a little more creative; because when our brains are constantly being entertained, they aren't necessarily busying themselves making new ideas.

The book's exercises included commuting without our devices, deleting addictive apps, going full days without taking photos, and just sitting in public places while staring out at the world—all in the name of letting our minds wander.

For the grand finale of the book, we were instructed to identify an aspect of our lives that we were confused by, avoiding, or downright terrified to think about. It could be large or small. Then, we had to sit down for thirty minutes, completely free from distractions (though we were allowed to watch a pot of water boil, which I did). When the thirty minutes were up, we were to list or draw or write out a solution to the problem we'd started with.

For me, it worked. My conundrum was finding a way to stay in touch with my friends and family in a manner that didn't feel overwhelming and that I wouldn't give up on after two days. Sending out mass emails seemed impersonal and like too much work. Facebook came with too many distractions. With the exception of three or four friends, nobody I knew ever wanted to talk on the phone anymore. I stared at my pot of water and let my mind wander. And then, after thirty minutes, I sat down and wrote. What I came up with was "a single sentence." To be more clear: I decided that I'd text a single line to a different friend every week. All it had to be was a line, like "Remember our imaginary dog in college?" It could turn into a longer thread, but it didn't have to. The only goal was to spend a moment thinking of a friend and to let that friend know. It's now been years, but I still try to text a single sentence to someone at least once a week. (And yes, I see the irony in the fact that my *Bored and Brilliant* breakthrough involved a screen.)

Jolenta also found her mind drawn to creative places when she put down her device. Without the distraction of her screen, her thoughts gravitated toward old creative outlets, like the piano, which she started playing again with some success. In the absence of Instagram feeds of dogs, she looked at real-life dogs and asked questions about how they navigated the world. And when it came time for her to attend the wedding of a dear friend, she didn't even feel tempted to take out her phone to take a photo during the ceremony. Instead, she chose to completely live in that magic moment. The experience made her happier.

Now, *Bored and Brilliant* isn't the only book we've lived by that suggests cutting down on technology usage. Tim Ferriss's *The 4-Hour Workweek* (which was filled with both good and bad advice) suggests setting aside only a few times a day to do things like check email. The rest of the time, Ferriss suggests leaving an out-of-office-style message explaining that there may be delays in response time.

Ferriss's reasoning is that choosing only certain times to be online will cut down on how much dillydallying and distraction we fall into so we can spend more of our lives doing the things we really want to—like learning a foreign language, starting a business, or mastering the art of horseback archery, as he did. And Jolenta and I certainly found we had more time (though I admit that I did cheat on this one a bit because, hey, I love to work).

Of course, not every book we've lived by suggests putting down our phones. One in particular, called *Pantsdrunk,* encouraged us to pour ourselves a glass of wine, take off our pants, lounge on the sofa, and scroll through social media as a way of recharging. *Pantsdrunk* author, Miska Rantanen, didn't see phones as demons at all (though he did advise against going on certain websites or answering work email).

Jolenta, an introvert, found *Pantsdrunk*'s advice restorative. She loved having permission not to be productive and to feed her brain candy.

I, on the other hand, found it sad-making. As an extrovert, sitting alone and drinking while reading (sometimes unkind) social media comments from listeners made me miserable. While *Pantsdrunk* didn't set out to make me put down my phone, I learned from living by it that I'm far happier drinking if I ignore my phone and spend time with friends.

One last thing worth mentioning here: None of the books we've lived by have told us to go cold turkey on our device usage. They haven't tried to kill our addictions. Rather, they've attempted to train us to use our devices more strategically and with more thought. The books all seem to accept that devices are a part of modern life and are impossible to sever ourselves from completely.

I tend to agree, though I do sometimes miss the days when most of the world was phone-free. I liked sitting at a dinner table where people weren't constantly checking their social media. I liked not worrying about other drivers texting or playing video games on the road. I miss the days of sitting in movie theaters where the worst transgression of those around me was whispering or making out, not Candy Crush and Snapchat.

I suppose this is just my way of saying that not only am

I happier when I spend less time on my devices, but I'm happier when the people around me spend less time on their devices as well. Unless, of course, I'm texting a single sentence to a friend. Or looking at eBay while sitting on the couch next to my husband with the TV on.

LIVE BELOW
YOUR MEANS

Kristen

When I was quite young—still in grade school—my parents got divorced. My father landed quite comfortably in the home of his soon-to-be second wife. Meanwhile, my mother went from working one retail job to three. The only way we survived was with my Nanna's free child care, groceries, housekeeping, and cooking—as well as the leftover food my mom brought home from one of her jobs.

In time, with my mother's second marriage, money become slightly less tight. But I was still expected to have a job and pay for everything from my maxi pads to my school pictures out of my own pocket. When I went off to college, I—like my mother before me—began working three jobs in order to pay the tuition bills and rent. I brought home food from the restaurants that I worked at that was destined for the trash. I squeezed my classes between my shifts. On more than one occasion, I bounced a check.

All that money stress took its toll. Well into my thirties, I carried a fear of homelessness inside me. And not just homelessness—but a whole imaginary scenario that involved two babies, a cardboard box, and drinking turpentine straight from the can.

Part of what helped me to deal with that fear was living below my means. And I learned from the best. My Nanna, who grew up during the Great Depression and was orphaned at a young age, was the queen of living well on less. She shopped garage sales, used the same tea bag all day, and kept every container of every prepared food she'd ever bought to use as "free Tupperware." She didn't have a lot of knickknacks and she didn't buy anything for full price. If you complimented her on her dress or sweater, she'd invariably respond by saying how much she'd saved on that dress or sweater (a habit that I also have).

The other thing that helped me tackle my turpentine fears was, quite frankly, making more money. From the ages of seventeen to twenty-five, I never earned more than $22,000 per year at my salaried day jobs—which is why I always waited tables and worked other jobs on the side. In my thirties, I started to earn more, but I continued to live as though my salary was still $22,000—putting a large percentage of my paychecks in retirement and savings accounts.

Now, I know we live in a world where living on less is considered the opposite of sexy. Shopping is one of our greatest pastimes. Owning stuff indicates success. McMansions, gadgets, and trendy fashions are supposedly central to our happiness. Choosing to live below our means really means saying no to a lot of the messages we're fed from the time we're babies. But more and more influential self-help authors are suggesting we do it.

The first book to really send this message to Jolenta and me was *America's Cheapest Family Gets You Right on the Money,* by Steve and Annette Economides. Over the first twelve years of their marriage, the Economides family lived on an average income of $35,000. During that same time, they paid off their first home, bought a second home twice the size of the first, and bought several cars for cash. They did all this through dozens of tricks, which included purchasing only secondhand items, not owning credit cards, and grocery shopping only once per month in order to cut down on gas money and impulse buying.

I mostly loved living by the Economides method. It made saving money feel like a game and shopping feel like a frivolous waste of time and money.

And while Jolenta didn't love the book quite as much as I did, it helped her to face her anxieties about money for the first time in her adult life, which led to tough but important conversations with her husband and even learning to log on to her bank account for the first time.

But for the most part, *America's Cheapest Family* presents only the most basic financial reasons for living below our means—so that we can have a home, a car, and a retirement fund. Other books present more exciting and/or emotional reasons.

For example, in *The 9 Steps to Financial Freedom,* Suze

Orman suggests that living below our means can help us to feel emotionally in control of our money (rather than the other way around).

In *The 4-Hour Workweek,* Tim Ferriss suggests that we can all lead more interesting lives if we spend less money on material items and more on low-cost experiences (some of which may even earn us money). One way of doing this is by temporarily living in a less expensive country than our own and working remotely while renting out our home for profit. Although neither Jolenta nor I did this while living by Ferriss's book, my husband and I have since rented out our home when we've traveled, which has helped pay for our trips.

In *The Life-Changing Magic of Tidying Up,* Marie Kondo presents another reason for living below our means— because owning lots of things also means the potential for lots of clutter. Clutter is a source of frustration for many of us—especially when it is made up of things that we don't need or love. Why not just hold on to the things that spark joy, and bring fewer items into our homes after that?

And then, of course, there's Bea Johnson's environmental argument for living below our means. In *Zero Waste Home,* she tells the story of how she and her family once lived the suburban American dream with a big lawn, a three-car garage, a giant house, and lots of objects to fill that giant house. Her family consumed gallons of bottled water every week, thoughtlessly purchased single-use plastics, and reassured themselves that—because they recycled—they weren't really damaging the planet.

In her early thirties, Johnson started to see her family's wasteful habits for what they were: destructive to the planet. After that, she and her family made a decision: They would be better stewards of the earth, and they would begin at home. They started walking rather than driving whenever possible, moved to a much smaller home, and shopped only for what they needed (while avoiding anything packaged).

Among the main pieces of information that Jolenta and I took to heart while living by her book was that refusing to purchase or accept things (even free things) was the most powerful thing we could do on a daily basis for the planet. We could say no to straws with drinks. We could refuse bags at the grocery store. We could say no to turning up the heat or turning on the air conditioner. We could say no to taxis and fast fashion and new gadgets and long showers. And we could refuse to buy anything in a package—even if the package claimed to be recyclable—because the vast majority of recycling programs in the United States do very little recycling and use a tremendous amount of resources in the process.

We could live with less. We could live below our means. And in the process, regardless of a book's primary motivation in telling us to do so, we found one common side effect: We were able to live more in the moment. When we focused less on things, we could focus more on people and experiences. When we learned to stop chasing more stuff, we could learn to be grateful for the stuff we already had. And when we pared down what we owned, we could better understand what we didn't need, what we did, and what truly made our lives better.

Dear Kristen and Jolenta,

It's great to live below your means, but what if you hardly have enough means to live on in the first place?
—SH

Dear SH,

You bring up such a valid point. The fact is, 12.3 percent of Americans live below the poverty line, according to the U.S. Census Bureau, and millions more people around the world barely scrape by. Living on less is absolutely not realistic for everyone. But my point in this chapter was not to suggest that everyone follow in my footsteps. Rather, it was to illustrate how budgeting (even during my poorest years) has kept my money anxieties from completely taking over my life, and in some cases, has even made me happier.
—Kristen

DECLUTTER

Jolenta

When the decluttering book *The Life-Changing Magic of Tidying Up* first came out and became a global hit, I scoffed at it. How could something so simple as the idea of putting your stuff away be that life changing? Part of my resistance was just a reaction to the sheer popularity of the book. I pride myself on liking quirky, unique objects, not the same dumb stuff everyone else likes. But not unlike my experience with a popular book series about a young man going to wizarding school, when I finally read what lay in those popular pages, I was sold. Turns out some stuff is popular for a reason . . .

Marie Kondo is a Japanese organizational consultant whose method of decluttering is known as KonMari, a combination of her last and first names. *The Life-Changing Magic of Tidying Up* has sold millions of copies globally.

According to Marie Kondo: The long-game goal of tidying isn't simply having less clutter; it's also about making us happier, and living only with the items that truly spark joy in our lives. And in order to appreciate the things that are important to us, we have to toss out the things that have outlived their purpose.

This may sound simple, but trust me, it's not. It's a ton of work. Kondo says to effectively figure out which of your belongings "spark joy" within your soul, you need to take one or two whole days to do a deep clean to get rid of any belongings you have that may be holding you back or are unnecessary. And to make things even more complicated, you can't just go from room to room seeing what you want to get rid of. Kondo says to go by category of belongings, because categories can be spread across various rooms.

Kondo says the best sequence for starting your decluttering cleaning journey is this: clothes first, then books, papers, miscellaneous household items, and last, mementos. So when we lived by this book back in season one of By the Book, I did just that.

I started by dumping every article of clothing I had into a pile on the bedroom floor, and picked up each individual garment, from my wedding dress to my gym socks. This took an entire day. It was exhausting. I loathed it. Cleaning my clutter was going to be the death of me. I started hating every item of clothing I picked up after a few hours, and had to keep going on walks around the block to clear my head and cool down so I didn't end up throwing out every article of clothing I owned.

But after slogging through the first day, going through other belongings became not only easier but also more satisfying. Halfway through day two of my deep clean I had a breakthrough. When Brad and I got to the miscellaneous electronics category, we gathered up every electronic device, charger, USB drive, plug adapter, and pair of headphones we could find and spread them all out on the bed. And to our dismay we saw we had a shocking number of obsolete electronics and accompanying accessories. The charger for a digital camera I no longer own, a binder full of hundreds of CDs Brad burned during his first year of college, and probably a hundred random odds and ends that we didn't even know we owned.

It was gross seeing so much of this useless garbage all in one place. Most of that junk had been with each of us since before we started dating years ago, some of it had even moved with us across the country from our childhood homes in Oregon and California, dragged from apartment to apartment for over a decade. After seeing how much unnecessary stuff we had cluttering up our little lives, we started understanding why we were doing what we were doing.

After that moment, tidying up literally began to feel kind of magical. Seriously. As corny as it sounds, I started liking it more and more. Downsizing everything we owned felt freeing; finding a place for everything we kept was like putting together a sexy-ass puzzle made out of all the things I love.

I hated the decluttering process at first and grew to love it. To this day, Brad and I say *The Life-Changing Magic of Tidying Up* is the one book I've lived by that made life better for

both of us. We loved the results of downsizing our possessions and unloading all the old belongings we'd been carrying around with us like dead weight. We can't get enough
of bare counters and efficient storage hacks. We love how
clean, bright, and calm our decluttered home has become.

Kristen's experience was pretty much the opposite. She
started with optimism and attacked her deep clean with
the kind of midwestern gusto only Kristen has. She felt ac-
complished as she made piles of clothes to donate and got
rid of old home workout tapes. But as time went on, the
more she and her husband, Dean, went through their stuff,
the more tension grew.

Kristen and Dean rarely fight. They get along so well
you'd think they're a happy-go-lucky couple from a made-
for-TV movie (before the new nanny they hire tries to take
over Kristen's life, that is . . .). But the way Marie Kondo told
them to arrange their home put them on edge, made them
tense, and made their lives superinconvenient. Things they
needed by the sink or in the shower were not next to the
sink or in the shower; they were hidden away in boxes and
cupboards. Tools they needed by the stove weren't next to
the stove; they were in drawers beyond reach.

It was maddening for them both, and in order to cut
down on their bickering and get back to their happy made-
for-TV norm, they slowly scaled back their extreme minimalism and let some choice clutter reappear throughout
their home. As they found their decluttering balance, Kristen began to notice that all of her and Dean's belongings
were much more integrated than they had been before.

You see, Kristen moved into Dean's apartment when they started living together, so everything she brought with her was crammed wherever it would fit. It wasn't until they took the time to get rid of excess and reorganize what they owned that she realized she could feel even more at home where she was living.

Overall, finding time to take stock of what I own and what I actually want has improved my life every time the idea has popped up in a self-help book we've lived by. When we lived by Anuschka Rees's *The Curated Closet,* a few seasons later, Kristen and I loved purging our wardrobes and defining our styles. While we lived by *Big Magic* by Elizabeth Gilbert, I decided to amp up my creativity by giving my office a makeover. I sorted, got rid of needless papers and other random things that didn't need to be there, and reorganized the furniture. After clearing out the clutter and implementing new systems of order, my office went from a disorganized room where we threw our coats to the place that I work in and enjoy all the time. I'm even sitting and writing this story in the damn room right now!

Through various forms of decluttering, including a huge deep clean and smaller-scale closet and office tidying sessions, what I've really noticed is this: The space around me is an extension of me. And just like me, these extensions of my existence deserve love, respect, and care. Decluttering helps me reconnect to myself, check in with who I currently am, and get rid of any old baggage that might be holding me back.

But Kristen and I learned the hard way that extreme

decluttering is definitely not for everyone. It was even a difficult process for me, and I ended up loving it. So don't worry about going balls-deep if you want to begin getting rid of clutter in your life that's no longer serving you; you can start with an office, a closet, a junk drawer—but not unlike that wizarding book series I mentioned at the top of this story, it's definitely worth a try.

Dear Kristen and Jolenta,

It seems that only a person who's well-to-do can really celebrate downsizing. People who genuinely live hand-to-mouth have so little already.

—SJ

Dear SJ,

You make a super good point. And I wish we had touched on this idea more when we lived by this book for the podcast.

A lot of the literature out there on decluttering and wellness in general seems to be written for people with the luxury of the means and time to hold each of their belongings to see what sparks joy. And that doesn't even include the money that comes with inevitably having to rebuy something you accidentally decluttered but still need, despite its inability to light your heart afire with passion.

But what have really continued to make my life

more enjoyable since initially decluttering are the organizational systems that are part of the process. You don't necessarily have to throw things out to feel that the space around you functions more smoothly and sparks more joy.

I enjoyed experimenting with Kondo's advice on how to store and categorize the paperwork and letters I had around my apartment. That cost nothing. And now I always know where to find my blank checks or the dog's vaccination records. My husband, Brad, years later, still folds his clothes in little spirals like the book recommends. He didn't get rid of many clothes, but he loves how happy looking into his closet makes him and how easy it is to see every garment and pick what to wear every morning. So you can still totally play around with aspects of minimalism and decluttering without having to sacrifice any of your belongings. And you only try it if that's something you want to do. Decluttering is totally not necessary to live a happy life, but for some of us, it can help.

—Jolenta

TRY NEW THINGS

Jolenta

With my aforementioned aversion to adventure, trekking, and all things wanderlust, you'd think I hate trying new things. And until recently I would have agreed with you. I too thought I hated trying new things until we lived by a book called *Year of Yes*.

Year of Yes follows TV writer and producer Shonda Rhimes's yearlong journey to say yes to everything that came her way after her sister told her she said no to everything.

The book digs into some of the reasons and excuses that Shonda gave for so long for saying no—from social anxiety to fear of embarrassment to simply being an introvert. And it shows how saying yes can help make life more enjoyable in the long run, and is in fact a necessary part of growing, learning, and becoming a better person.

Living by *Year of Yes* was a pure joy for Kristen and me. We each said yes in our own ways, and it enhanced both of our lives. I said yes to coffee with a new friend, hosting a party, hosting a women's networking event, and getting a foot rub. I even said yes to dressing my dog up as a squirrel and taking him to a costume parade.

Kristen said yes to spending time with loved ones when she made the effort to see a friend who was in town from London. They caught up on each other's lives, spotted a Real Housewife of New York out on the town (hint for you *Housewives* fans: *Turtle Time*), and since her friend is a freelance podcast host and she had just transitioned to freelancing, he ended up giving her some great advice on next steps. His input led to Kristen saying yes to starting a freelancer club so she didn't lose her mind with boredom while learning to work in a less social environment.

One of the coolest things about living by *Year of Yes* has come in the form of the slow realization that I'm actually kind of good at saying yes to new things. (Duh, I literally cohost a podcast where I try new things every two weeks!) In fact, saying yes to something new is how basically everything I love has come into my life. Saying yes to taking one storytelling class is how I eventually found my way into doing stand-up comedy. Saying yes to hanging out with a goofy acquaintance is how I ended up married to Brad. I bet if you look back at your life, you'll see there are lots of badass, brave yeses you've said to new things that took you places you never imagined you'd go. That's very cool, if you ask me.

You can even say yes when things feel out of control; Kristen is the perfect example of this. Right before we started living by *Year of Yes*, Kristen was informed that the podcasting company that employed her full-time was shutting down and she was about to be unemployed. This time was hell for her. But saying yes to new things here and there helped her make the most out of a less than ideal situation. She said yes to asking for help and sent emails to freelancer friends in the industry whom she admires asking if she could meet up with them and get advice. She found a community for herself and created a freelancer co-working club with a few friends.

Kristen also worked on her brand. She plugged her website like a beast and submitted herself for speaking engagements and podcast guest spots. She threw herself into saying yes to every new thing that she could think of or that came her way. And in doing so, she turned getting fired into embarking on her kick-ass solo career. Within months of being fired and all the new things that came with that, Kristen was hosting a podcast at a new company, guest-hosting others, and even writing her own book, *So You Want to Start a Podcast;* so she had a lot to say yes to.

Since we read *Year of Yes,* I've started being able to see my life as a series of brave choices to try new things. And if trying new things usually leaves me feeling like I've got a list of badass accomplishments in my wake, then I guess I'm pretty into trying new things. As long as those new things aren't trekking; I still say no to that . . . (Sorry, Brad).

RECHARGE

Jolenta

My alone time is sacred. When I say "alone time," I'm not talking about masturbation (okay, sometimes I am talking about masturbation). I mean time spent on my own doing something relaxing, indulgent, or even mind-numbing.

I always credit my love of quiet solitude to the fact that I'm an only child. I've been chilling on my own since day one. But until recently this wasn't cool. For the majority of my life I've felt that my need for a little me time to replenish my energy was a weakness.

Our society tends to idealize extroversion. We often equate successful people with outgoing, supersocial personalities. I was under the impression that people like me, who need to remove themselves from the world and rest in order to thrive, would never be as successful as those who don't have this weakness.

Fortunately I was wrong about this. In the past few years there has been an introvert revolution. The self-help shelves are flooded with books about how to essentially stay in, eat, drink, light a candle, and relax your way to happiness.

When we lived by a book called *Pantsdrunk,* which promoted this kind of introverted recharging, I was as happy as a pig in poo. The Finnish concept of *kalsarikänni* (pantsdrunk) centers on relaxing at home in your undies while drinking and with no intention of leaving the house. Indulging in a pantsdrunk evening is supposed to help recenter you after long, stressful days and give you a chance to partake in the ease of "meaningful meaninglessness."

I was overjoyed to see this advice in a book. Finally, a way I already take care of myself is validated as something other people think is worth trying—and even writing a book about! Within seconds of finishing the book I had cracked open a bottle of rosé apple cider, turned on a Lifetime movie about a cyberstalker, and got my recharge on.

By the end of our two weeks living by *Pantsdrunk,* I was a master of all things revitalizing and indulgent. I experimented with eating bags of chocolate chips while watching Real Housewives marathons and texting funny GIFs to my best friend while I sipped a beer and did a face mask. I was staying in, pampering my ass as hard as I could, and loving every second of it. Even Brad noticed I was in a way better mood every morning after I took an evening to get my pantsdrunk on. It was the real deal.

But the deal was less real for Kristen; her experience was not as blissful as mine. The combination of activities just didn't work for her. Drinking alone made her sad. Reading negative comments on social media while under the influence bummed her out and made her feel lonely. And no matter how hard she tried to pantsdrunk, she often found herself feeling more stir-crazy than recharged.

Kristen is an extrovert; she gets energy from being around other people. Socializing doesn't suck her dry the way it does me and most other introverts. She recharges by having a group of friends over, or by wandering off to the farmers' market. And that's just as valid as chilling with a glass of wine in an old oversize T-shirt. Because recharging and taking time to replenish your energy is what is good for you, no matter how you do it.

What I really loved about living by *Pantsdrunk* was the permission it gave me to actually indulge in how I naturally tend to unwind, instead of feeling guilty for watching "garbage" TV or staying in to have a fancy snack instead of going out on a Friday night. We all deserve this kind of permission to treat ourselves to time that is free from obligations and expectations. And no matter how you do it, taking care of yourself isn't a waste of time.

So when you need to recharge, own it any way that feels right for you. Grab that wine and an old movie and cuddle up with your dog on the couch. Host a karaoke party with all your friends and sing until the sun comes up. Or grab your favorite "alone time" toy and go to town on yourself. You deserve it.

Dear Kristen and Jolenta,

I find that when a lot of people say they want to recharge, what they really mean is that they want to go to a spa or salon, or do some online shopping, or put on expensive face masks while drinking rosé.

In today's world (and especially in the self-help world) isn't *recharge* just a code word for consumerist self-indulgence?
—LS

Dear LS,

Your findings are definitely real. It's frustrating that general concepts like "wellness" and "recharging" have been co-opted by social media influencers and consumerism. Selling recharging crystals or shilling face masks in the name of happiness is hollow and takes advantage of people truly searching for more in their lives.

But I like to try to believe that all advice, at its root, is sincere. To test this theory, I always try to see if I can live by a book while spending as little money as possible. I've found that recharging (via pantsdrunk, hygge, or any other means) can easily happen without purchasing a thing.

I found that, while reading books on how to recharge didn't change me or my habits much, it did help me reframe how I already relax. I'm able to see it as necessary and good for me. Something I can do with intention instead of see as a lazy vice.

But lots of people aren't me, and I think advice on staying in to revitalize oneself may work better for those of us who identify as introverts. It can help take away some of the guilt we introverts usually associate with needing alone time to recharge.

I know many extroverts (Kristen included) who go stir-crazy taking this advice and choose to relax in very different ways. These ways to unwind are fun concepts that can help you kick back, but they aren't hugely life altering, and definitely not worth spending tons of money on—you've got that right.

—Jolenta

GO OUTSIDE

Kristen

I am proudly and unapologetically a city person. I hate be-ing too far away from mass transit. I love being surrounded by other humans. The idea of living in a cabin in the woods miles from civilization is my worst nightmare.

But it's not just that I love cities. I love the indoors. I love being on this side of a window screen while bugs are on that side. I abhor pooing in a hole in the ground that I was forced to dig myself. I think the inside of a movie theater is one of the most magical places on earth.

Even when I was a kid, my parents would sometimes have to yell at me to go outside.

"Get your nose out of that book!"

"You've watched enough TV!"

"Stop building that bomb shelter under the basement stairs! You've already amassed enough canned goods!"

(I blame the tail end of the Cold War for that last com-mand.)

That being said, once I got outside, I usually had a glo-rious time. I loved riding bikes with my friends and going on picnics with them and collecting flowers and caterpillars that we would raise into monarch butterflies. I loved playing tag in backyards and climbing all the playground equipment in the summer. I loved ice skating and building snow forts and sledding in the winter. I loved knowing (during those last glorious days in the eighties when grade-school-age kids were allowed to disappear for hours at a time) that my friends and I could get up to all sorts of no-good as long as we were home by the time the streetlights came on each evening.

And from a young age, I loved going on walks—whether around a Minneapolis city lake with my mom or just from my house to a friend's house a few blocks away.

The outdoors was full of possibilities and space to roam. Sometimes I just needed the urging to get out there.

As I grew older, I was urged less and less. Tests needed to be studied for, papers needed to be written, I had to get to my after-school jobs.

And once I hit adulthood, it wasn't just that I had no one reminding me to go outside. The world had changed into a place where we never had to leave our houses to see one another or entertain ourselves. There was the Internet. There was Skype. There was Netflix. Even when I moved to New York—the city that ostensibly never sleeps—I found that people loved to stare at their devices as much as take on the town.

On top of that, the outdoors became more and more commodified and commercialized and seemingly out of reach for someone of my modest means. Hundred-dollar shoes and fifty-dollar canteens were suddenly required for an amble in the woods. Bikes that cost more than my annual rent seemed mandatory for cruising around with friends. High-performance outerwear replaced old T-shirts and beat-up shorts for anyone who just wanted to go for a jog.

And in the midst of all this, the one outdoor activity I'd always loved—going on walks in my city—was suddenly deemed "not an outdoor activity." The outdoors industry (and SUV manufacturers and energy bar makers and a large swath of self-help influencers) made it clear that if you were surrounded by skyscrapers, you weren't really enjoying the outdoors.

So even though I was still spending time outside and walking every day (and up to twenty miles per day on the weekends), I was doing the outdoors wrong, in the wrong clothes, and in the wrong location.

But if I was doing it all wrong, why did I still enjoy it so much? Why did wandering around for hours surrounded by tall buildings as an adult give me so much of the same joy I felt exploring the outdoors in my suburban Minnesota development as a small child?

There are a lot of answers one could give here. Maybe it's because, as I mentioned in the chapter about putting down our devices, it gave my mind a chance to wander without a screen. Maybe it was, as Jolenta touched on in the Try New Things chapter, that walking sometimes took me to new places and gave me new experiences. Or maybe I just got joy from moving my body.

But I'm going to argue here—contrary to the views of

some outdoors enthusiasts—that even on my city streets, I was getting a rejuvenating dose of nature. I was surrounded by more sky than I could get inside my apartment. I felt the wind on my face and the sun on my skin. Even with 8 million neighbors, I heard birds chirping. And for every four-lane road I walked along, there were fifty tree-lined brownstone blocks filled with squirrels, front gardens, and flowers.

According to Florence Williams, my theory might actually hold weight. In her book *The Nature Fix,* she says that the colors, patterns, smells, sounds, and textures of nature make us calmer, more empathetic, more positive, more creative, more focused, and healthier. What's more, she insists we can enjoy the benefits of nature even in the most urban settings—which is exactly what I did while living by her book.

My husband and I walked through city parks and smelled the flowers. Each day, we admired our city birds—from sparrows to starlings to pigeons. We planted two gardens— one on our balcony and another, for growing herbs, inside our living room window. And I, in a truly unusual move for me, began taking a few minutes away from my desk several times a week to look at the leaves on the plants in the square outside my office and enjoy the clouds rolling by.

All these activities made me feel an amplified version of what I already felt on my long walks through the city. But as much as I loved having my life choices validated by Florence Williams, I also want to make something clear: I don't think my belief in *The Nature Fix* was based just on confirmation bias. To illustrate this, let's look at Jolenta's relationship to nature and her experience with the book.

Jolenta grew up in Portland, Oregon, at the edge of the city, with a forest and a creek in her backyard. To her, nature has always meant sitting on the side of a babbling creek and watching the birds while smelling the rain beneath a canopy of ancient trees. When she goes west to visit her family, she always makes time to be by the ocean and go hiking.

But when we lived by *The Nature Fix*, Jolenta didn't have the time or budget to just hop on a plane to the West Coast. She and her husband were in the midst of moving to a new apartment. They were dealing with packing and organizing and setting up a new home and all the other logistics that go into relocating.

Thus, Jolenta had to force herself to experience nature in a new way. Instead of sitting by a babbling creek in the woods, she sat on her fire escape at tree level and listened to her neighbor's backyard fountain. Rather than walk through a forest, she and her husband hugged the tree outside their apartment building. And whenever she had a free moment, she tried to find the nature of New York City hidden in plain sight.

And here's the thing: It all made her happier. A few minutes of fresh air made her feel calmer during her move. Hugging that tree outside her building with her husband made her feel more thankful for where she lived. And finding flowers growing out of the concrete made her pause and appreciate the world more.

Of course, no book is perfect. Jolenta and I both question Williams's claims that nature can cure ADHD or PTSD or nearsightedness. And her assertion that we should all go on at least one multiday wilderness vacation per year shows a lack of awareness about most Americans' economic realities.

But that being said, Jolenta and I have found that going outside makes us feel happier and calmer—whether the outside is on a fire escape, along a Minnesota lake, or on the edge of an Oregon forest. Look around. Breathe it in. There's a huge, joyous world outside the bomb shelter, my friends.

Dear Kristen and Jolenta,

I just want to point out that the great outdoors doesn't make everyone happier. Some of us have allergies to nature and are susceptible to sunburns and also hate the cold and bugs and pretty much everything else in the outside world. Personally, I'm much happier sitting on my couch and watching reality TV than I am on a nature trail. I'm an indoors person!
—IP

Dear IP,

We get it. Jolenta and I both have allergies to all sorts of outdoor things—from pollen and ragweed to the cold (yes, being allergic to the cold is a real thing; it's called cold urticaria and I have it).

On top of that, we've both been known to get injured outside—suffering bug bites, sunburns, blisters,
and scratches. There was even that one time that I
got dragged out by the undertow at Fire Island, which
resulted in my back being torn up by seashells and a
sense of panic I've carried with me ever since, every
time I'm near truly wild water.

Yes, the outdoors can be rough. And we don't pretend that it's for everyone. In fact, when we talked to
Florence Williams, author of *The Nature Fix,* she even
said that about 5 percent of people really and truly are
legit indoors people. But she also pointed out a couple
things:

1. Many of us who think we're indoors people are in
   fact inertia people. Wherever we are, that's where
   we're comfortable staying. And since modern
   urban and suburban life mainly centers on the
   indoors, that's where the inertia tends to keep us,
   unless there's some intervention (like a parent
   dragging you out of your pretend bomb shelter).
2. Even indoors people tend to benefit from an open
   window and some daylight. Even indoors people
   tend to like the look of a blue sky or stars or the
   feel of a light breeze. And even indoors people who
   want to watch reality shows on the couch all day
   like to see the occasional scene of people or animals outside.

We're not trying to convince you to go outside. We're not even trying to convince you to watch more nature programming. You do what feels good to you. But to us, what feels good is a bit of the outside from time to time, even if the outside is just an open window.

—Kristen

SAVE THE
WORLD

Kristen

Week after week, book after book, for years now, Jolenta and I have done what our self-help authors have told us to do: We've written about our feelings and thought about our dreams and fixated on our anxieties. We've decorated our homes and labeled our personalities and recited mantras while rubbing lotion into our bodies. We've looked at our bedtime routines and eating routines and tracked just about any behavior there is to track.

And at a certain point, we began to find it all a little counterproductive and narcissistic.

This isn't to say that Jolenta and I are opposed to self-care. Quite the opposite. We think it's important to know ourselves, to seek help when we need it, and to celebrate all the good and unique things that make us who we are. We believe in finding ways to be kinder to and more accepting of ourselves. All these things are important.

But too often, the bestselling books we live by stop there. They look inward, but not outward. They give tips on how to self-soothe, but they don't address many of the issues that cause us to need soothing in the first place. And, just as bad, they imply that if we feel unhappy in a lousy situation, it's because of us, not the situation.

What if we started trying to change the situations instead? What if we stopped focusing on just our hurt feelings about the world's injustices and started fixing the world's injustices? Would we feel happier?

Jolenta and I dabbled in these questions when we lived by Jill Neimark and Stephen G. Post's *Why Good Things Happen to Good People*. And we dove in even deeper when we lived by Emma Gray's *A Girl's Guide to Joining the Resistance* and Bea Johnson's *Zero Waste Home*.

Girl's Guide in particular helped us to tap into our inner activists. The book begins by encouraging readers to consider what they give a fuck about in this world—whether it be racial or environmental justice, women's and LGBTQ rights, or any number of other issues that affect us. And during this step, readers are encouraged to tie in their own stories. For example, have you had to face sexism at the doctor's office? Maybe this means you want to ensure that all women have access to better reproductive health. Have you personally faced the negative impacts of air pollution and climate change? Perhaps earth justice is what you want to fight for. Have you been profiled specifically because of your race? Maybe it's time to fight for racial equality.

I decided that environmental justice and racial equality were the main things I gave a fuck about—partly because I felt these issues affecting me regularly, but mostly because it broke my heart (and continues to break my heart) to live in a world where racism and environmental destruction are widely accepted norms.

One might presume that the book's next step is taking action, but in fact, it's listening: listening to people whose stories are similar to ours and different, listening to people who don't look like us and whose voices are often ignored. I particularly loved this step. It led to deeper conversations with some of my black friends about the daily decisions they have to make in order to avoid police violence. And it also led to uncomfortable but important conversations about my own privilege—privilege that has nothing to do with being white or wealthy (I'm neither), but that affords me advantages nonetheless.

By the time we got around to taking action, Jolenta and I felt ready. I got to know which candidates running for office had records of supporting racial and environmental justice. I mentored young women of color who wanted to become journalists. I spoke up when I saw people of color being mistreated. I reported businesses that left their doors wide open in the summer to lure in customers with their AC. I went to my local community garden and asked how I could help out. I cleaned up trash on the sidewalks. I donated to one of my favorite environmental organizations. I called the governor to voice support for environmental legislation. And I used whatever platforms I had to help the world and its inhabitants.

As for Jolenta, she took steps to fight for gender equality. That meant writing a piece about the PE teacher who sexually harassed her in high school. It meant talking to the heads of that school. It also meant attending women's social justice events and learning more about all the ways that misinformation—particularly about reproductive health—was hurting women.

Admittedly, our efforts led to different personal outcomes. Jolenta felt a slight increase in her anxiety about the state of the world. But that anxiety was far outweighed by a sense of strength. To quote her, "I felt more empowered than ever in the face of sexism and other biases that usually seem so overwhelmingly big. I used to feel paralyzed by the idea that little old me couldn't do anything impactful enough to make real change." But living by *A Girl's Guide to Joining the Resistance* took the paralysis away.

I've actually found that fighting for justice alleviates my anxiety a bit. The more I volunteer or donate to environmental causes, the less I feel I don't deserve to be on the planet. The more I volunteer with diverse teens, the less fear I feel about the future world they'll grow up in. And the more I stand up for others, the more I believe it's possible that others will stand up, too.

To be clear, neither Jolenta nor I thinks we can save the whole world. We're just two people. But maybe we'll make one person's day a little better today, and another person's tomorrow, and another's the day after that.

And in the midst of these tiny steps, she'll feel a little more empowered and I'll feel a little less anxious—and isn't that so much of what self-help is about?

PREPARE
TO DIE

Kristen

Jolenta is extremely fortunate in that very few people she's
loved have died so far. But on the flip side, she's also unfor-
tunate. She's the only child of two parents who live in different states, many time zones away, and she's well aware
of the fact that when they die, it will be on her to carry out
all their wishes, manage their assets, arrange their final
resting places, and settle all the legal matters that need to
be settled. It will be on her to feel the deep sense of loss a
child feels, without a sibling to share the emotions. It will
be on her to do it all, and it will be painful. And so, I suppose it's not surprising that Jolenta usually likes to avoid
the topic of death—her own or anyone else's. To her, death
is both a distant concept and a heavy burden.

And it's for this reason that I wanted to live by a book
about death for our show. I figured a lot of listeners were
in the same boat as Jolenta, walking the line between emotional avoidance and legitimate fears—both knowing that
death is inevitable and hoping it won't need to be considered for a long time. Sadly, in most Western cultures we

don't spend a lot of time talking about death or preparing for it. When it happens, it often hits us like an otherworldly event we never saw coming—even though, logically speaking, we all know that we'll someday die.

My husband, Dean, and I know this from firsthand experience. We've both lost parents and grandparents to whom we were quite close. And in both our cases, we've come to understand the importance of accepting and preparing for death.

Dean's father's death was sudden and unexpected, and it happened on the other side of the world, on the South Island of New Zealand, where he grew up. There was a lot of shock and pain to process. There was the regret over not having had the chance to say goodbye. And there was the logistical nightmare of taking four connecting flights across the world from the United States to be reunited with his mother, sister, and extended family.

Once Dean arrived, the emotional pain was exacerbated by the pain of realizing his father had never planned for his own death. His finances were not in order. His papers— most of which were impossible to decipher—were spread far and wide across his family business and home. At one point, Dean and his mother and sister considered bringing in a forensic documentation expert to help. In the end, after many tireless hours and a lot of agony, they managed to arrange a funeral and save the business. And all of this was on top of losing someone they deeply loved.

My mother's death was also a sudden and unexpected event. She had been fighting a severe cold for many months.

She'd also been acting not quite like herself. She seemed needier than usual, and I wasn't sure why. But I knew I'd be there in a few weeks, at the same time I visited her in Minnesota every year. I told her to take good care of herself until my annual visit. And I put my trust in my aunts and uncles and extended family—all of whom still lived in Minnesota—to drag my mom to the doctor if things got truly bad.

But then I got the call—my mother was in bad shape. She was in the hospital. I needed to get on a plane immediately. They didn't know if she would make it. I booked the first flight I could. The flight was delayed, and then delayed some more. The woman sitting next to me on the plane, hearing my story, said she'd get her husband to take me to the hospital when we landed. Thanks to that woman, whose name I can't remember, I made it in time to see my mother conscious one last time and tell her I loved her. She went into a coma that night.

As my sister, aunts, uncles, and I waited for the doctors to find out what was happening with my mother, I remained hopeful that there would be a clear diagnosis and an obvious course of treatment. But eventually, it became clear: My mother had metastatic cancer—and it had spread everywhere, including her brain. We could keep her in the coma for as long as we wanted, or we could disconnect her from life support and let her die. No one wanted to be the one to give the order to disconnect. But I remembered what my mother had always told me: "Please don't keep me artificially alive." And so I said out loud what no one else would: "Please disconnect her." My sister and aunt—who were my mom's legal proxies—delivered the order to the hospital staff. And then we all gathered around her, holding her and telling her we loved her as she died. This was only a year and a half after we'd done the same with my beloved Nanna, my mom's mom.

It was horrible. The pain of loss. My own guilt over not coming back to see my mom sooner, when she first told me about her extended cold. The angry sense of unfairness in having two people I loved so dearly taken away from me so close together. But unlike Dean, we had the advantage that my mother had planned for her death. She had an advance directive. She had a will. She had my sister and her sister assigned as executors. And she had told me more than once what she wanted to happen to her body when she died—that she wanted to be cremated, and that she wanted her ashes scattered alongside her favorite spot, at her favorite lake.

When we lived by *The Art of Dying Well,* by Katy Butler, Dean and I recalled our own stories of loss. We thought about what we considered a "good" death. We discussed what we wanted to have done with our own bodies when we die. We completed some important paperwork. And we talked about what we wanted our legacies to be. Both of us said we wanted the kindness we've shared with others to live on.

In Jolenta's case, living by *The Art of Dying Well* was quite different. It wasn't about focusing on losses she'd experienced but about confronting the fact that her parents would someday die. This meant having important conversations—

conversations that, in the end, were reassuring. While she was talking with her mom, it came to light that there was already end-of-life paperwork in order. It also became clear that Jolenta's mother wasn't afraid to ask for help, and in fact already had a team of people she relied on for her needs—including, to Jolenta's relief, an attorney.

In addition to beginning the process of considering her parents' deaths, Jolenta also began considering her own death—and what a good death would mean to her. She realized that she wanted an animal in the room with her when she died. She decided on a book passage she wanted read out loud to her in the end. And she talked at length with her husband about what "quality of life" meant to each of them.

In the end, both Jolenta and I felt better after living by Katy Butler's book. Jolenta felt less afraid. I felt more prepared. And overall, we both felt a little more in touch with the reality of death—as well as what we value most in life.

Dear Kristen and Jolenta,

Just hearing the word *death* makes me sad. Like seriously, I go into a panic when I think about death.

—MB

Dear MB,

I feel you. I'm in the same boat. I normally try to avoid confronting the idea of mortality at all costs. I even tried to back out of living by the one and only book about death that we covered on By the Book.

I'm never going to tell you to do anything you know will trigger you or make you needlessly sad. But I can say that my experience with getting uncomfortable and exploring what death means to me also helped me explore what life means to me. And that was a wonderful experience.

I went from totally avoiding the subject to realizing that I was more afraid of the unknown than of anything else. (And really, aren't we all?) But the more I got to know the unknown and define what it meant to me, the less scary the idea of death became in general.

Through planning for my death, I ended up having wonderful conversations with my family. I got a rare chance to carefully explore what I find wonderful, where my priorities are right now, and to connect with the people I love. So that wasn't too scary.

—Jolenta

PART 2

8

Things That Didn't Work

WAKE UP
EARLY

Jolenta

I'm not a morning person. At all. You could say early mornings and I are mortal enemies, and the same goes for Kristen.

Sadly, our society isn't very encouraging toward those of us who don't like early morning wake-up calls. Most of our prescribed daily routines, like when we have to go to work and school, begin early and celebrate those who naturally start their days at the crack of dawn. Because of this fact I've always wanted to fix my aversion toward mornings and learn how to become an early riser.

I had high hopes that a book we lived by called *The Miracle Morning* was going to finally teach me how to properly seize the day before noon. The author, Hal Elrod, posits that 95 percent of us are mediocre. Unlike the top 5 percent of people (based on what statistics I don't know), most of us won't retire comfortably, are overweight, and are headed for divorce if not already there. But we don't have to stay that way. We can have it all. All we have to do is choose to learn, grow, and be a little better each day by taking an hour or two every morning to write, sit in silence, exercise, list affirmations, and visualize what we want out of life. Truly, that is it. Get up early and do a handful of generic "wellness" activities and you'll be as successful as Cher selling the first affordable tickets to vacation on the moon.

This sounded incredibly doable. And all I want to do, ever, is stop being mediocre. So after reading the book, I set my alarm for seven o'clock the next morning (instead of my usual 9:00 A.M.) and got to work, or should I say sleep? As I drifted off into dreamland, I fantasized about all the things I'd get done in my early mornings. I was finally going to write that thirty-minute comedy set. I was going to become mindful because I would finally have time to sit in silence. It was going to be great.

But the work of being early to rise didn't go smoothly. No matter how early I tried going to sleep, Brad had to wrestle me out of bed in the morning because I would sleep through my early alarm. When I finally did wake up, every activity was torture. Sitting in silence was impossible; no matter how I tried, I kept falling right back asleep. One morning I started nodding off during my silent time and woke up to my hair on fire. I had lit a candle for ambience and managed to dip my hair in it as I passed out. I was fine, just a few crispy, smelly burned ends on a little chunk of tresses. While I wasn't injured, I was sorely disappointed. Starting my day with the smell of burning hair didn't leave me feeling miraculous.

By the end of the first week I was a mess. I was totally sleep deprived and underperforming in every area of my life. I was lackluster at work and in the sack. And eventually I just got sick, retired to my bed, and gave up on living by the book.

After a week of sleeping, coughing, and blowing my nose nonstop, I had finally recovered from living by *The Miracle Morning*. And I'm here to tell you it didn't work for me. Which sucks, because Hal Elrod basically promised me it was the one surefire way to get my life in order and start being more productive. It's almost as if one scheduling hack really blew a dude's mind and he decided to build a whole brand around it before checking to see if it was universally true (which most things aren't except, like, gravity).

Waking up early made me far more mediocre than I was when I got up at my usual time. And even though she didn't get sick, Kristen also hated getting up early. She struggled to stay awake and had many late-night work events that made getting up early almost impossible. Eventually she gave up, too.

And I don't blame her! She already had what I would consider to be the perfect morning routine. Her husband, Dean, wakes her up as late as possible by rubbing her feet, and then she tosses on some makeup and runs out the door. Why mess with what works? Kristen is definitely not mediocre, so maybe getting up early to do some randomly prescribed "wellness"-related activities has no bearing on how successful you are.

I've learned this the hard way: You can't fight your internal clock. Sleep is necessary, and you can't hack it or bypass it too much without ceasing to function properly. I think everyone has a miracle hour, that one hour or two a day when you always seem to crank out your best work and deepest thoughts with ease. That hour is probably around 6:00 A.M. for Hal Elrod, and that's why he thinks getting up early is the best way to be productive. But there's no one time that's best for everyone. Who really cares if you like centering yourself or being productive at midnight, noon, or 4:00 P.M. The time doesn't matter. Now quit worrying about how to optimize your morning and go back to bed.

Dear Kristen and Jolenta,

I understand that you don't personally enjoy waking up early. But waking up early really and truly does work if you're willing to do it! Why do you think so many high schools start their day at 8:00 A.M.? Why do so many gyms have yoga classes at 6:00 A.M.? Why is the U.S. Army's motto "We do more before 9:00 A.M. than most people do all day"? Because starting the day early means getting more done! I speak from experience as someone who rises at 5:00 A.M. each day.
—ER

Dear ER,

We totally believe you when you say that waking up early helps you get more done. Congratulations on finding something that works for you! Unfortunately, the same is not true of us. Jolenta and I have found that our energy levels are not especially high in the mornings. We don't produce more work or get more done just because we're up earlier. If anything, we're grouchier and more exhausted and more susceptible to illness.

That being said, we get plenty done when we do eventually get out of bed. We write and host our two podcasts. Jolenta does stand-up and storytelling shows and also has a full career as a voice-over artist. I teach classes and consult companies that want to start podcasts and host other podcasts, and until last year, I headed up a whole department of a podcasting company. We work a lot. And we get a lot done. Look! We're writing a book right now!

But we understand why some people feel that early risers get more done. The fact is, the world is set up for them, as you yourself have pointed out, ER. This means that people who love waking up early have the advantage of being able to go to school and fitness centers at an hour that feels good to them. It means they can be productive when the world tells them they should be productive (rather than at 10:00 P.M., when Jolenta and I are often typing away).

Enjoy your early hours, ER! Enjoy that the world is set up for you! Get everything done that you want to! Jolenta and I will get our work done later tonight, when you're fast asleep.

—Kristen

MEDITATE

Kristen

Friends, before you insist that I absolutely must meditate, that it's scientifically proven that all people should, that I don't know what I'm missing, that I'm probably not the best version of myself because I don't meditate, let me just get this out of the way: You are more than free to enjoy meditation. And I'm not ever going to try to stop you from doing it. If that's what you love doing, have at it.

But I will not be joining you. I hate meditating. I hate sitting still concentrating on my breath. I hate closing my eyes and trying to push all the thoughts out of my head. I hate quieting my mind and settling my thoughts while my legs and arms are in positions that someone else tells me they need to be in.

Trust me, I've tried. I've tried in the past on my own and in classes. And I've tried with many of the books that Jolenta and I have lived by. The most notable of these was *Meditation for Fidgety Skeptics*, by Dan Harris, Jeff Warren, and Carlye Adler.

Now, Jolenta figured that *Meditation for Fidgety Skeptics* would be the perfect book for me. Unlike *The Miracle

Morning, it didn't ask me to wake up at an ungodly early hour to meditate. And unlike other books we've lived by, it didn't ask me to meditate with the goal of getting rich or being more forgiving (I have zero belief that meditation can lead to the former, and I have no interest in doing the latter). On top of that, it was for skeptics like me, so it had to be a good fit, right?

Wrong. For the two weeks we lived by the book, I did not find myself happier. Meditating made me more tense, not more calm. It made me aware of all the things I could or should be doing, rather than giving me a way to zone out. And on top of that, it connected me with the most single-minded, judgmental proselytizers I'd ever met.

Whenever I told meditation lovers I wasn't enjoying meditation, they would insist I was doing it wrong. Whenever I said it wasn't for me, they'd say it was for everyone. Whenever I said I'd tried it dozens of times and still didn't like it, they'd say I needed to try it hundreds of times before I would.

"Everyone hates it at first," I'd be told. "But eventually, after many hours, you will reach a place of peace."

Here's the thing: I'm already a pretty peaceful person. I raise my voice only when people are about to walk into traffic or about to hurt me. I very rarely spiral into negative or anxious thoughts. And I'm great at living in the moment. Eavesdrop on me as I walk down the street, and you'll find me talking to each squirrel and smelling every flower as I revel in the feeling of the wind on my face. I'm fully in the moment.

And when I'm meditating, I'm not. I'm wishing I was walking down that street with those flowers and squirrels, or dreaming of seeing friends, or laughing about something funny that happened to me that day, or maybe just drifting off to sleep. I'm doing none of the things with my brain that meditation says I should be doing. And when I try to guide my brain back to what I'm being told to do, I'm not having fun.

I have a few theories about why I don't like meditation. One of these theories comes from my friend Eric Sasson. As he sees it, I'm wired like a good-natured windup doll. Each morning I wake up fully wound and ready to do a million things. I march around, happy and productive and playful, and then as the day winds down, so do I. And then I go to sleep and let my body and mind restore themselves. The next morning I wake up fully wound again.

"You do, do, do, and then you sleep, sleep, sleep, and you get all the energy and restoration you need from those two things. You're just not wired for meditation."

Another theory I have is that meditation might be better suited to people who are trying to tackle specific challenges that (fortunately) aren't a regular part of my life. For example, Dan Harris began meditating as a way to treat his anxiety and addiction issues. Other people, he points out, use meditation to manage their feelings of rage or to help them develop impulse control. Perhaps if these were ongoing issues in my life I'd love meditation. But since they rarely are, meditation tends to feel like surgery for an ailment I don't have. And as our original By the Book producer Cameron

Drews once said, "Nothing makes Kristen as unhappy as a book that tries to fix something in her that's not broken."

A final theory I have about my dislike for meditation is related to my identity and personal history. As a woman of color who also happens to be an abuse survivor, I've been told way too often in my life that being quiet and being still will make things better—when that absolutely has not been the case. And I abhor the idea of self-styled gurus telling me otherwise—especially when those "gurus" are white men whose books I've had to live by. What's empowered me most in life has been speaking out and standing up. What's made me feel less afraid and more in control is being anything but quiet. And what's made me feel more connected with each moment has been getting out of my head and more into the world around me.

Whatever the reasons, I don't like meditation.

Jolenta is a slightly different story. When we lived by Harris's book, she did see some real improvements in her life. When she found her anxiety or anger leading to negative thought spirals, she'd pause to say her newly adopted mantra—"I'm a queen bitch, and I've got this shit on lock"—and doing so would help derail her normal thinking patterns and reset her mind. When she felt the need to practice more compassion, the exercises in the book helped her tap into that part of herself. And when she wanted permission to relax, the book's lazy meditations—which can be done on the sofa in front of the TV—put her in a state of bliss.

That being said, Jolenta also found that some of the book's exercises frustrated her, bored her, and made her physically uncomfortable (note to everyone out there: Some meditation postures are super stiff-making). She didn't love everything about meditation. She certainly didn't see it as the be-all, end-all solution for humanity. And boy did she get tired of hearing from all the meditation zealots who kept insisting it was the solution for all the world's problems.

Of course, if you're a meditation zealot (or even only a meditation dabbler), I just want to reiterate: You are free to meditate. I hope it brings you joy. But it's not for me. And it's only sometimes for Jolenta.

Dear Kristen and Jolenta,

You're just wrong about meditation. It is being introduced to some schools and hospitals and prisons because it really helps people stay centered during stressful and often life-threatening situations. It helps to cut down on violence and anxiety. If you don't like to meditate, you just don't like science.

—KW

Dear KW,

I totally agree with you and science; the benefits of meditation are real. And if it works well for you that is awesome! I'm jealous.

For Kristen and me, it felt taxing and frustrating as opposed to enriching. And while we may be in the minority, we aren't going to stress too hard because

I think we've found other ways to get the benefits of meditation in our lives.

Kristen loves walking through the city to get into a state of flow before work. I love to center my mind by crocheting at night. We have our ways, and even if they aren't as powerful as simply sitting our butts down and meditating, they work for us.

Also, if you want an expert's opinion, here's a letter from a clinician-listener on the subject:

I'm a clinical psychologist and I practice and teach mindfulness meditation. From my experience of my own mindfulness practice, I see amazing benefits to meditation, but I would still query the assertion that everyone needs to meditate. There are two things I think most people need to have in their lives, and mindfulness meditation can be a great way to get them, but it is by no means the only way.

Thing one: the ability to shift into a "being" state of mind, present in the moment, instead of always and only existing in "doing" mode. "Doing" mode isn't necessarily getting stuff done but distraction and overthinking and disappearing into the past and future and hypotheticals and worries and obsessions. A "being" state of mind is being fully engaged in the present moment.

Thing two: the ability to step back from your thoughts and emotions, notice what's going on, notice patterns and what does and doesn't work for you, and make decisions about how to respond or make changes without feeling overwhelmed. Some people just do this naturally; most people have some way of doing this, through journaling or painting, or talking with a supportive person who can say, "Hey, you've got caught up in that same thing again; let it drop."

I don't want anyone to think that if they can't spend two hours a day opting out of normal life to meditate (like Dan Harris does), they have to miss out entirely on something that is available to everyone and for free. —E
—Jolenta

ADMIT YOU
ARE A LIAR

Jolenta

When I was a little tyke of only four, I was a big ol' liar. A blatant, OshKosh-B'gosh-overall-wearing, bald-faced liar. Whenever any adult at my play school asked my name, I told them it was Laura.

Even at the tender age of four I knew my name was "unique." Every time I introduced myself I'd have to listen to a chorus of people saying things like

"Oh what a *different* name."

"Wait, how do you pronounce that?"

"Whoa, weird name."

I was over being "different" after a few weeks of this. So I picked a beautiful, common late-eighties name, Laura, and started telling everyone who asked that that was what I was called. It was a lie. I knew the truth, picked a name that didn't correspond with said truth, and opted to tell people that nontruth.

That is lying. Knowingly choosing to deceive someone. Lying to people usually isn't nice or worth it. When the truth comes out, the person who was lied to often feels betrayed and hurt, unless the lie is about a surprise party or present or something . . . those are okay. But as I was saying, lying is a choice, and it usually makes everything worse. When I lied about my name, I embarrassed every other parent who went up to my mom asking if she "belonged to Laura." And it could have been even worse than that. What if I got hurt or there was an emergency and the parent volunteer was frantically looking through the play school directory for Laura's emergency contact because little baby Jolenta wanted to lie that day? You catch my drift—don't lie. It's not worth it unless you are lying about giving someone you love a cool-ass surprise.

Why am I ranting about lying? Because self-help books love to call their devoted readers liars. The most blatant example of this came in season four, when we lived by Rachel Hollis's book *Girl, Wash Your Face*.

Hollis grew up the youngest of four kids in a white, working-class, insular, evangelical Christian community. She describes her childhood as both sheltered and traumatic, and she was desperate to escape. So, at the age of seventeen, she graduated from high school early and launched a new life for herself in Hollywood. Within her first two years there, she landed a job with Miramax, rubbed elbows with wildly famous people, and began dating the man who would eventually become her husband.

Now, Rachel Hollis is the founder of her own event-planning company, the creator of a hugely successful blog, and the author of several books. In *Girl, Wash Your Face*,

Hollis insists that her trajectory can be replicated if we simply choose to be happier and stop lying to ourselves. And she insists that if we're unhappy, it's our own fault.

To illustrate her point, she lists, chapter by chapter, the twenty biggest lies she used to tell herself—and the ways those lies kept her from being her happiest self. Along with those lies, she lists the steps she took to rewrite a happier script for herself—steps that she insists we can all take on our journeys to greater joy.

The lies she lists include the following:

- Happiness comes from outside factors.
- I'll never be good enough.
- I'm always right.
- My love life defines my self-worth.
- I'm a bad mom.
- I'm not smart enough.
- I'm not sexy.
- I won't be worthy of love until my body is the right size.
- My trauma defines me.
- I need to drink/do drugs/self-destruct to cope with life.
- I need someone to come save me.

This list is full of self-destructive sentiments; I'll give it that. Holding on to these negative beliefs will definitely detract from anyone's quality of life. And these mean things should not be believed or adhered to if you want to enjoy life and not hate yourself.

But here's the thing. These are categorically *not* lies we've made up to tell others or ourselves. This isn't like randomly choosing to start telling people your name is Laura when really it's Jolenta. It's not our fault these false and denigrating beliefs have seeped into our brains and inserted themselves as hard-and-fast rules—we didn't arbitrarily choose these lies that hold us back from enjoying ourselves and our lives. Picking up self-limiting beliefs isn't the same as strolling through a meadow and plucking any passing flower that catches your eye. I think it's a bit more complicated than that.

These lies are instilled by society. Our cultural value systems are often invented by advertising, large corporations, and consumerism—and they implant these self-doubts and false truths in our heads. And they've done this for one simple reason, if you ask me: to prey on our insecurities and get us to buy more things to fix all the problems they say we have.

You didn't create these lies that rotate through your head denigrating you every day. These lies were presented as truth by the powers that be. You are not stupid for buying into them and perpetuating them. I truly don't believe any book should blame you for being influenced by lies instilled in you by others. How dare any book have the balls to give us a hard time for buying into the lies constructed by others and presented to us as truths? That's literally vic-

tim blaming. Telling people they are responsible for the social inequities and biases that hold them back in life is just
another way of keeping oppressed people down and in no
way promotes self-care or living life to the fullest. It's also
pretty lazy advice. From what I can see, Hollis found what
worked for her and then generalized that advice, saying it
could help anyone from any walk of life. And obstacles that
she'll probably never encounter as a white, straight, con-
ventionally attractive woman are written off as "self-limited
thinking."

This insidious message pops up in many other books,
too. I touched on this when I was talking about *The Miracle
Morning,* a book that insists the best way to start your journey to self-betterment is to admit you're a mediocre person.
When Kristen and I were living by Mark Manson's bestselling book *The Subtle Art of Not Giving a F*ck,* the first step
we had to take toward giving zero fucks was to take responsibility for everything that's occurred in our lives, regardless
of whose fault it was initially.

According to Manson, we don't always control what happens to us, but we can always control how we interpret what
happens to us, as well as how we respond. It's that simple!
The more we choose to accept responsibility in our lives,
the more ownership we're supposed to feel.

Fuuuuuuck this notion. Not only is blaming yourself for
the actions and beliefs of others superdepressing, but Kristen and I have also found it to be quite self-destructive.

We came head-to-head with this blamey self-help theme

when we lived by *The Four Agreements* by Don Miguel Ruiz. In the book Ruiz lays out four rules or "agreements" to live by. These agreements help us see the self-limiting beliefs that hold us back from joy and push us toward freedom, true happiness, and love.

The second agreement that Ruiz recommends we all live by is this: Don't take anything personally. He says what others do is not because of you, it's because of them. Because of this, it should not be important to you if other people think you're the most magical sparkle pony in the world or the smelliest of all the garbage people. How people react to you isn't your problem either. If you living your life makes someone say, "You're hurting me!" that's on them, because they're letting themselves be hurt by you.

Although I take things personally, like all the time, when I first read this I was on board. Taking things personally does feel bad, and I don't like feeling bad. And often it really just is miscommunication. But then I started looking at what taking things personally gets done—it changes laws, it changes lives. Protests and movements come from groups of people taking injustice personally. It felt like more advice that existed to oppress the already disenfranchised.

The thing I hated most about this step was watching how it hurt Kristen. She hated this advice more than anything else we've encountered while living by a book. Kristen is the amazing, joyful, inspirational, seemingly perfect person she is because she's worked really hard to understand that any pain inflicted on her during her childhood was *not* her fault. This step was asking her to undo all of this hard work and blame herself for being a helpless child, one who was never asking for the abuse that came her way.

What a cruel task to advise in the name of wellness.

I think we take things personally because they are, in fact, personal. Even when they aren't intended to be, who cares? Damage has been done whether the perpetrator meant to inflict it or not. I'm sick of feeling ashamed for this whole "it's only business" lie—everyone has feelings, and everyone takes things personally sometimes. What if the time we spent punishing ourselves for feeling feelings were put to a better use? Perhaps that energy could be spent on personal healing or considering the feelings of others. Personally, I'd rather try to learn from my pain and maybe prevent others from feeling similar ills than blame myself for the random acts that have hurt me throughout my life.

The whole time we were living by *The Four Agreements* I kept thinking about that PE teacher I had in high school who tortured me by ridiculing my body and manhandling me—that felt awfully personal, it definitely personally affected me, and I have every right to take it however I want. In fact, it's freeing to say how much I took it personally instead of telling myself I'm dumb for being bothered when a person in a position of power took his garbage out on a powerless kid.

Any advice that tells you it's your fault you were fed lies about your worth and lovability is bad advice. And for people like Kristen, who have busted their asses to move past trauma and abuse at the hands of family members and authority figures, this advice can be retraumatizing.

As Kristen wrote in her verdict when we lived by *The Four Agreements,* "It's insane to expect . . . people to open all [their old] wounds back up and then say, 'Hey, it's not the abuser's fault! He didn't know any better!'"

You're never to blame for things beyond your control that hurt you or put self-deprecating beliefs in your head without your consent. The societal inequities, racism, body shaming, sexist beauty standards, and other roadblocks put in place to maintain social and economic structures are to blame. Most of these lies have been around in some form or another for generations. So no advice book should ever tell its readers to shoulder the responsibility for these boring old lies.

Instead of blaming ourselves for the deception of others, I wish more books helped us explore how to get to the root of the self-limiting stories we tell that hold us back. Maybe then we can find the actual root of that lie, get mad at it, and pull it out like the gross weed that it is.

But also, please don't lie.

Dear Kristen and Jolenta,

I just want to point out that authors like Rachel Hollis come from an Evangelical Christian background, and in Evangelical Christianity, it's vital that we acknowledge our own sins, wrongdoings, and yes, lies. Doing so is the first step to being a better person. Repentance is central to the faith.

—EC

Dear EC,

We're absolutely not opposed to repentance. We all do things wrong—with other people's feelings and with our own responsibilities. Why, just yesterday I got short-tempered with my husband—not because he'd actually done something offensive, but because I was hungry and grouchy. And of course, afterward, I apologized—because when we behave badly we absolutely should repent. For more of our thoughts on this, please see our chapter "Offer Gracious Apologies."

That being said, Jolenta and I also believe there's a difference between being repentant when we've done something wrong and using "I'm a big fat liar" as the jumping-off point for improving our lives. It's blamey. It's judgey. And depending on how we look at things, it's very likely not true.

Too many self-help authors—both Christian and not Christian—do this. And when they do, it's hard to feel as though they're not negging us—in other words, breaking us down, only so that they can build us back up—and then selling us a boatload of expensive online classes, life coaching, and conferences afterward. In the case of authors who call on their religion in the process, it can also feel blasphemous, disingenuous, and predatory toward those of the same faith.

Of course, it's possible that some of these authors genuinely do see themselves as liars, and absolutely believe they must admit their lies in order to enter the kingdom of heaven. If that's the case, fine. We don't

want to take their religion away. And, EC, we don't want to take yours away either. But Jolenta and I aren't part of the same faith community. And we won't be going around calling ourselves liars anytime soon.
—Kristen

GO ON
A DIET

Kristen

I'm going to say something completely unscientific right now that I 100 percent believe to be true: If diets really and truly made people happy, every woman in America would have been happy many times over before reaching the legal drinking age. That's because we've all been on diets, or been told to go on diets, or had diets explained to us or advertised to us on a loop from the time we were old enough to absorb information.

For me growing up, the message was unrelenting, especially from the people who loved me. My mother and aunts were constantly on fad diets—from the grapefruit diet to the cabbage soup diet to the white rice diet to every major brand-name packaged food diet. When they managed to drop a few pounds, they celebrated. When the weight inevitably came back, they'd lament. Not long after, they'd find a new diet to follow.

Nanna, while not technically a dieter, was always very persnickety about her weight and others' weights. She got on the scale each morning. She prided herself on wearing the same dress size her whole adult life. She constantly commented on people's figures and "problem areas"—whether those people were on TV or at the grocery store. The women in her own family heard her commentary the most. A week rarely went by without her saying, "Are you really going to eat *all that*?"

Like a lot of people who grew up in households like mine, I realized very early that my weight was something to fixate on—and to fix. And popular media—from magazines to TV to toys—just drove this message home. I was supposed to hate my body. I was supposed to put in the work to make it lovable. The way to make it lovable was to restrict what I ate. But inevitably, I'd fail and have to start over.

And boy, did I do it well. From the time I was in third grade, I tracked what I ate and counted calories. I compared my body to those of other girls, including my wire-thin older sister, to whom I am not genetically related and thus have no reason to see as a realistic basis for comparison. I starved, then binged, then threw up. I smoked instead of eating, or I ate bags of food that I hid. I weighed myself a minimum of three times a day. During one spring in high school, I lost thirty pounds, which was nearly 25 percent of my body weight. The women in my family were thrilled. So was I.

My food and body issues continued off and on through college. My weight fluctuated. My starving and bingeing and throwing up came in cycles. I tried diet pills and anything else I could get my hands on.

And then, I graduated from college and moved from Minnesota to New York. Gradually, I started to fixate less on my weight. Maybe the shift was because I was farther from the women in my family and their constant talk of weight. Maybe it was because I no longer owned a TV or had magazine subscriptions that yelled at me to be on a diet. Or perhaps it was because I suddenly had friends in a much wider variety of sizes who loved their bodies and whom I found beautiful.

More than likely, it's also because I began talking at length with a counselor about the other reasons I'd felt bad about myself before heading to New York. I'm guessing it's also simply because I was so excited to be in a new place, starting a new life, with the chance to be anything I wanted—including a million things more interesting than the number on a scale. And on top of all that, New York also gave me the chance to appreciate my body as much for what it did as for what it looked like—every day, my legs took me up and down hundreds of subway stairs and across miles of city sidewalks.

I really can't say for certain what put a halt to my dieting, my bingeing, my purging, and my constant obsession with my body. I'm guessing it wasn't any one thing. But I can say this—I was so much happier once I stopped fixating on my weight. I had so much more free space in my head when I wasn't constantly counting calories. The world felt bigger and richer when I gave it more attention than I did the size of my thighs. And more than anything, I felt an overwhelming sense of relief to be off the hamster wheel of failure.

And yes, that's how I see diets: as hamster wheels of fail-ure. Diets don't take you to a destination. They keep you on the same cycle: hate your body; decide to fix your body by making it smaller; go on a diet; when someone questions your diet, deny that it's a diet and explain that it's a "life-style" or "eating plan"; lose a little bit of weight; gain weight back after no longer being able to keep up with the diet; feel like a loser; start over.

Note that part about lying about your diet. I think that's because, deep down, we all know diets don't work, so we're not supposed to say we're on one. We're just naturally sup-posed to be skinny . . . because . . . skinny is better? Skinny means you're smarter? You're more worthy of love if you're skinny? More in control? Sure, tell that to my bulimarexic seventeen-year-old self.

The truth is that there's no inherent value in being a skinny woman. I know this. Jolenta knows this. And in their hearts, I think most human beings know this. But diet books are everywhere, and in the spirit of trying to cover all the different kinds of self-help bestsellers, Jolenta and I once tried to live by a diet book. It was called *French Women Don't Get Fat,* by Mireille Guiliano, and in the big wide world of bestselling diet books, it seemed as if it would be one of the least harmful. According to the blurbs, it was about embracing the joy of eating, not counting calories. It was about savoring tasty bites of good things rather than eliminating whole food groups. And above all, it wasn't about dieting!

And so, when Jolenta and I had each put on a few pounds

after the holidays during the first season, we decided to give the book a go. We knew people wanted us to try a diet book, and what harm could be done in two weeks?

Turns out, a lot.

We began with tracking what we ate. Every meal, every snack, and every beverage. And even though the book told us only to weigh our foods rather than track the calories in them, I found myself falling into all the old habits that tracking used to include for me: I began calculating every calorie, as well as every category of food that passed my lips. Was it a carb? Or was it a protein? Tracking food soon morphed into tracking my activities. How many calories was I burning each day? Was I burning off enough? Maybe if I walked just three more miles.

And of course, we weighed ourselves. The book says not to be a slave to scales, but we figured listeners would want to know what we weighed at the beginning and end of living by the book, and so we weighed in. But then I weighed myself a second time to make sure the number was right. And then again and again and again. Within a couple days, I was weighing myself dozens of times a day, including secretly when I found bathroom scales at friends' houses. Sure, it was obsessive, and it was exactly what the book told us not to do, but was weighing myself really that different from weighing my food?

This was followed by what Mireille Guiliano calls the "Tough Weekend." The book instructed Jolenta and me to boil leeks and then consume the water the leeks were boiled in. If we got really hungry we could eat some of the boiled leeks themselves. And if we got insanely famished, we could even dribble a tiny bit of olive oil on the boiled leeks.

I didn't want to submit to the leeks or the oil. I wanted to be strong. But halfway through the Tough Weekend, I reached a breaking point. So rather than eat the leeks or the oil, I cheated by eating a lettuce leaf and two pickle slices. I began crying. I was barely into the book and already failing.

When the Tough Weekend ended, we were again allowed to eat—but the diet was full of oil and dairy and meat, three things of which I'm not especially fond. Did I mention I don't like French food for the most part? I don't. Also, I'm lactose intolerant.

And on top of that, the book instructed us to eat at times of the day when I usually don't, and restrict food at other times when I usually do. Specifically, the book said we were required to eat breakfast, lunch, and dinner and forgo bedtime snacks. Now, I don't eat breakfast and I never have. From the time I was very young, my preference has been to sleep in as late as possible, run out the door, and then, after building up an appetite for a few hours, eat lunch. In the evening, I eat dinner. And before bed, I usually have a bedtime snack of broccoli, popcorn, or something else that's crunchy.

In other words, the book was asking me to upend my entire eating schedule. Suddenly, I had to wake up earlier and force-feed myself when I wasn't hungry. And once I started force-feeding myself, my appetite got weird. I was hungry all day long, every minute of the day. And my mind was constantly fixated on food—from what I ate to when I ate to how much I ate. And throughout all this, I was weighing myself as often as possible.

Partway through week one, I called Jolenta crying because I was in such despair about breakfast. She insisted that I just break the rules or modify them.

"Hey, I do it all the time! And in your case, all you have to do is rename your lunch, dinner, and bedtime snack so that they're called breakfast, lunch, and dinner."

I did as she said, but I was still driving myself crazy. All I could talk about or think about was food. I had a crazed look in my eyes. I began building my entire life around what I could and couldn't eat. At the end of the first week, my husband called an intervention. He knew the book was doing very bad things to me. He begged me to quit.

After many tears, we came to an agreement—which he didn't actually agree upon. I decided I would follow the book only in the loosest way possible. I felt a duty to finish it—if only partially—so that we could demonstrate to our listeners how damaging even the most "healthy" eating plans can be. I was committed, miserably so.

As for Jolenta, she had a slightly easier time of things. Prior to the book, she'd had a habit of mindlessly eating entire boxes of cheese crackers in a single sitting. During the book, she checked in with her body more, noting when it was actually hungry and what it actually wanted to eat. But overall the process was still needless torture for her. During the end of the Tough Weekend in particular, she cried with delight when she allowed herself a few drops of olive oil on her boiled leeks. Let's be clear: No one should be weeping with joy because they starved themselves for a whole weekend and then consumed ten calories' worth of oil. No one should be starving themselves in the first place.

At the end of our two weeks, Jolenta and I each weighed in and found that we'd dropped a couple pounds. But, despite experiencing a few benefits, Jolenta didn't feel the diet was healthy. And what I lost in weight was more than overshadowed by the trauma I felt during those two weeks—and in the weeks that followed. As we moved on to the next book and the next book after that, I continued to track my food and weigh myself up to fifty times a day, sometimes getting up over a dozen times in the middle of the night just to do so.

And despite all the obsession, the weight came back. A few weeks later, I weighed more than I did when the whole experiment began. And of course, I felt horrible about myself.

"Are you really going to eat all that?" I heard a voice in my head saying—a voice I'd quieted years before.

What had I done to myself?

Dear Kristen and Jolenta,

Some of us really like to be healthy and fit. Some of us like to fit into our size six jeans. Some of us really do feel more confident in our bodies when we put our health first!

—GK

Dear GK,

You do you. As long as you are doing things with and for your body and health that you love, and that make your life better, I'm all for it.

What I'm not for is using the word *health* as a way of holding bodies to unfair and often sexist, racist, or any other *-ist* standards. As long as health and weight aren't considered synonymous, I'm totally fine with health. I love that kind of health. The kind that doesn't assume skinny is true health and knows that weight doesn't reflect one's moral failing or character strength in any way. That kind of health is great and keeps us alive!

But I don't love it when I'm advised to fit into a certain size or look a specific way so society will call me good-looking. That's not health advice; that's just an annoying opinion I didn't ask for.

—Jolenta

DEFINE
PEOPLE
BY GENDER

Jolenta

I've never considered myself to be "good at" relationships. The only real boyfriend I've had is the guy I ended up marrying. Before him, a very fun variety of long- and short-term friends with benefits paraded through my life.

Once Brad and I decided we were dating, I still sucked at relationships. I did so many rude, passive-aggressive, and ill-advised things that some days I truly marvel at the fact that we've managed to make a life together.

Here is a list of things I did in my relationship that I would now advise against:

- Starting as friends with benefits on and off for a year
- Kicking the person out of your house at 4:00 A.M. after hooking up and telling them, "I don't want my roommate to see you here, it's too embarrassing"
- Breaking into the person's email to read correspondence with people they dated before you two were exclusive

- Fighting with the person while cooking Thanksgiving dinner and throwing the whole pot of stuffing you're making onto the stovetop out of rage
- Working up the courage to agree to move in with the person only while coming out of anesthesia after surgery
- Secretly trying on the engagement ring the person is hiding from you in their bedside table to check the size, seeing it's too small, and dropping a billion hints about your finger size before they pop the question

Needless to say, when we decided to read a bestselling book about communication in relationships, I was stoked.

Men Are from Mars, Women Are from Venus, by John Gray, is one of the bestselling relationship advice books ever written. It came out in the early 1990s, when I was around six years old. I saw this book on countless shelves and coffee tables, and in baskets of reading material in the bathrooms of everyone's parents' houses. To me, it was a symbol of true adulthood.

I figured that once I read it I would finally be a real adult in a true grown-up relationship. And as I noted earlier, I needed all the help I could get to find more mature and functional ways of communicating with my partner. Sadly this wasn't the result.

Upon finishing the book, I was devastated. I ran to my (now) husband, Brad, fuming with rage, and the following exchange occurred:

JOLENTA: This book is saying, "Just deal with it—men are from Mars, like, he's a Martian"—while I'm saying I expect human things from both of us. And I don't think I'm being . . .

BRAD: Unreasonable?

JOLENTA: Unreasonable or one-sided or too much of a Venusian to expect you to live up to human expectations about living adult human lives. The book is all, "Do these quiet tricks, and let him learn on his own. He'll fly when he's ready." But it's like, he's my husband! He's not my kid. He's not my baby bird. He's not Martian! It's letting men off the hook. I feel like the book is just saying, "Yeah, pretend to listen to her so she feels validated." But it doesn't say to actually validate her, ever. It just says give her the impression you're validating her and then do your own thing. Where I'm like, can't (clap) a woman (clap) get some (clap) validation! Do you see what I'm saying?

BRAD: Yeah.

JOLENTA: Do you feel like I'm mad at you or, like, lecturing you?

BRAD [nods]: I feel very shut-down.

JOLENTA: *Why?* I'm just getting heated about this book, I'm not mad at you!

BRAD: Because your takeaway from this book is, Brad is wrong and I am right.

JOLENTA: No! My takeaway is that women are always wrong [voice starts to shake] and, like, no matter what you do [starts crying] you have to cater yourself to men and [fully crying now], like, the way they deal with things, and you'll never be heard unless you change everything about yourself [still crying gently].

BRAD: Change everything?

JOLENTA [mildly wailing]: That's what it's saying! It's like, "The way you communicate is wrong, and of course you don't get what you want [tears are slowing down] because you're an overbearing c*nt." It's a disappointing book, because I feel like it's just saying, "Jolenta, you're wrong." When I feel my whole fight in our relationship is to feel heard and validated. And then this book comes in and stomps on that, implying I'm crazy for wanting my needs to be met.

BRAD: I agree. It doesn't give women enough credit.

Instead of groundbreaking advice on how to clearly communicate my wants, needs, fears, and so on to my partner or tips for controlling my anger, the book was full of super-sexist pointers based on the idea that men and women are completely different species (and, in fact, aliens from two different planets). It has chapter after chapter excusing men.

Saying they're naturally shut-down and conversation-averse and shouldn't be expected to process or express emotions.

I find that generalization of this kind is rarely helpful. To me, it reads as an acrobatic theory used to imaginatively gloss over the fact that all humans are unique, regardless of gender (which is a social construct anyway), or any other idea that's popularly used to marginalize populations. It's easier to say, "Nature made us like this!" than it is to say, "Oh, weird, why do we seem to be socializing half our population to see working through emotions as weakness? It seems like this low expectation of maturity hurts those around them."

I want to investigate the problems I face in life and in my relationship. I do not want these problems reasoned away with sexist ideals. And surprise! Sexist advice doesn't just pop up in books about relationships. In *Pick Three,* Randi Zuckerberg posits the idea that pretending to have it all, while actually strategically balancing too many tasks behind the scenes, is the answer for women to find fulfillment. When Kristen and I read this we were disappointed that the book never really addresses the root of where these unfair expectations to "have it all" even come from.

Why not acknowledge that society tends to expect more of women? Women should be perfect homemakers, ultra-supportive of their spouses, involved parents, and employees who work as though they have no obligations waiting for them at home. Advice about how to fake having all of these things under control just furthers the problem. And maybe I'm naïve, but I want my self-help to help a lot more than that.

Dear Kristen and Jolenta,

I'm a baby boomer woman, and maybe it's just my generation, but men and women really are different. We were raised differently; we were taught to communicate differently; we were brought up with different social expectations and trained from day one to take on different roles. Considering all this, aren't men and women—at least in my generation—inherently different?

—OP

Dear OP,

We are all products of our environments and times. And yes, the time you grew up in was rife with hard-and-fast rules about what constituted a real man versus a real woman. Some of these roles are hard to move past. Some are so ingrained it can feel hard to distinguish between what's "inherent" and what's socially constructed. On top of that, even if you want to move past the gender roles you were raised with, you may find that other people around you don't. They may prefer that you stay the way you are, and they may want to stay the way they are, as well.

That being said, people change all the time, and society changes all the time, and even if we feel we're in a static, unmoving version of the world, we're not. Perhaps, OP, you attended a school in which girls always wore skirts and never trousers, but now you yourself are very comfortable wearing either. Perhaps you know a man your age who was raised to think cooking was for women, who now loves nothing more than making a good stir-fry. Change usually comes so slowly we don't see it happening. But it does happen.

One last thing: While the world treats gender as a given, it's not. Yes, we're born with the sexual organs we're born with, but those organs do not automatically mean that we'll identify as a specific gender. There are people with testicles who identify as women. There are people with vaginas who identify as neither a woman nor a man. Gender and gender roles are complex. And even if they feel like it, they're never inherent.

—Kristen

FORGIVE

Kristen

A very large percentage of books we've lived by have suggested that practicing forgiveness is essential to feeling happy and at peace. These books usually say that forgiveness is something we should do for ourselves, not for the people who did us wrong. By our forgiving, they insist, our wrongdoers will no longer take up space in our psyches, and we'll be released from the shackles of the past.

According to these books, forgiveness can take a variety of forms. In many cases, it's letting go of all the anger and pain we feel over being mistreated. In others, it's an act of absolution. Still others equate it with gratitude—as in, we can thank those who've hurt us because they played a role in making us who we are today. And in the case of Don Miguel Ruiz's *The Four Agreements,* it's making a concerted effort to see things from our abusers' point of view—abused children are advised to acknowledge that their abusers were victims of their own upbringing, and thus not at fault for their actions.

What I say to all this is "Hells no." And what Jolenta says can't be heard by the human ear, because the sound of a woman skipping past a step that says "forgive" (which is what she almost always does) is just that quiet.

Let's start with the pain and anger part. When bad things happen, I think people *should* feel pain and anger—the victims should, and the victims' loved ones should. Pain and anger are natural responses to injuries—both emotional and physical. And when we pretend we don't feel these emotions, we're in denial (at best) or sociopaths (at worst).

As I see it, anger gets a bad rap. There are many situations that justify it, and many situations in which anger pushes us toward greater action—like fighting for racial equality, or repealing laws that hurt women, or working harder to protect children, or walking away from people who are horrible to us.

To be clear, I'm not talking about rageaholic levels of vitriol that manifest in irrational acts of violence. I'm not talking about carrying around a fury so great that it's all you can think about most days. But in self-help books, we're often told that anger in any amount is dangerous— even a low-grade anger that sits mostly dormant ten levels beneath the surface. According to these books, any amount of anger eats us up and prevents us from being the best versions of ourselves.

Call me cocky, but I think I'm a pretty great version of myself. And I think Jolenta's top-notch as well. And we both have some anger. I have anger toward that former friend who repeatedly tried to get it on with my then-boyfriend a few years ago. Jolenta has anger toward the PE teacher who harassed her all through high school. And I most certainly have anger toward my father and his wife—who did all sorts of violent and disgusting things to me growing up. It's not the kind of anger we feel most weeks or even months. But it kicks in when we see someone else being hurt (if you want to see Jolenta get all Mama Bear, just hurt someone she loves), and I certainly feel it when I find myself in situations where I could be in danger. I consider it handy.

Let's move on to the form of forgiveness that's also called absolution. I'm totally okay with this form of forgiveness in most day-to-day interactions. For example, if someone accidentally steps on my toes on the subway and apologizes, I'll absolutely say "No worries" or "That's okay." Same goes for someone calling me the wrong name or showing up five minutes late or breaking a wineglass or making any number of other accidental mistakes. We all make mistakes. Who cares?

But when we're talking enormous transgressions, I'm not going to say "That's okay" or "No worries." It's not okay if you deliberately cause physical or emotional injuries to me or someone I love. It's not okay if you take my rights away because of my gender or race. It's not okay if you dehumanize me or other humans. And I certainly won't say "No worries" if you've instilled a horrible sense of worry in me over my own worth. Example: Are you someone who repeatedly told me I was useless in my most formative years? If so, I'll never say "No worries" to you.

There are a few arguments for the absolution model of forgiveness. One of them is the belief that if you say "You're forgiven" or "It's okay" or "No worries," you really and truly will feel it is okay and no longer be haunted by worry. Another is that absolving wrongdoers is an act of kindness that allows them a fresh start to try to do better. And, of course, there are those who believe that absolution allows for the slate to be wiped clean for everyone involved. Obviously, I don't agree with this. If something truly horrible was done, saying "It's okay" won't make it disappear. And in a lot of cases, I don't want wrongdoers to have a fresh start. I want them to think long and hard every day about what they did wrong and feel remorse. Jolenta, for her part, feels this even more strongly than I do.

Do not cross Jolenta.

Now let's talk about the gratitude version of forgiveness. Should we be thankful for everything that's made us who we are today? Proponents of this model say yes, because surviving adversity means we can relate to other people who've survived adversity. It also means we can tap into more complex parts of ourselves. But I think there are limits to this idea. Yes, some adversity can make us more empathetic and nuanced in our thinking. But then take that adversity up a level and I'm not so sure. Is it really making a person better, or worse?

Frankly, I wouldn't wish some of the abuse I've faced on anyone, much less my younger self. I'm not grateful for it at all. And for all the supposed good things forgiveness proponents will say I gained from it, I can name dozens of bad things I also gained—from confusion about healthy ex-

pressions of love to demented ideas about my own worth—
things that took me years of counseling to come to terms
with. And Jolenta sure as hell isn't grateful for the abuse
she's suffered either.

Finally, let's talk about understanding. If we try to understand the people who've done us wrong, will we be happier?
If we see their bad behavior as the result of bad things that
they had to live through, will that bring us peace?

In some cases, I think this can be true. For example, if
someone—hypothetically speaking—steals a loaf of bread
from my store because they're desperate and hungry, those
are circumstances I can understand and forgive. If someone bounces a couple small checks to me because they were
brought up with absolutely no understanding of money
management, I can forgive that. And if a person's transgressions are nonviolent, I can also usually enlist my understanding.

But for me, it stops there. I would never expect a rape
survivor to try to understand her assailant's point of view.
I think it's downright cruel when people think rape survi-
vors should.

And my feelings on this go both ways. Just as I would
never extend understanding to a child predator, I wouldn't
expect others to draw on their understanding if the predator was me. I wouldn't want them to say, "Hey, she was
treated badly growing up; it was inevitable she'd hurt someone else." Growing up in a lousy situation doesn't give a
person carte blanche to pay it forward. And while some

people choose to continue a cycle of abuse, the vast majority of us don't. Passing it on is not an inevitability.

Now, at this point, you may be thinking: *Holy smokey, Kristen is a coldhearted, unforgiving monster. She sure must be unhappy with all that bitterness in her heart.* And to that, I say: Surprise! I'm actually superhappy. I've said it before and I'll say it again: I have a song in my heart and a spring in my step, and more often than not, I have a jolly smile on my face. I have close friends like Jolenta and beloved family members and my dear husband, who would drop anything and everything to help me in a moment of need (they all have). I see beauty in the world every day. I am the opposite of bitter.

And no, I don't carry around the pain of my past like an albatross. I'm not dragging around a ball and chain of rage. I don't feel I'm being held hostage by past trauma. I don't feel I'm held back in any way by my refusal to forgive certain things or people.

As my friend and founding By the Book producer Cameron Drews once wisely said, "There are a lot of options between unconditional forgiveness and burdened misery. We don't have to choose one or the other."

Indeed. We can choose not to wish any happiness on the people who've done us wrong *and* live happy lives. We can choose not to feel grateful to the people who've hurt us *and* be grateful for the lives we have. And we can choose to have some anger in our hearts toward those who've abused us *and* still have hearts that overflow with joy.

The world is filled with in-betweens, and I honestly believe life is better when we don't force ourselves to live on the extreme ends. If you want to, go ahead. But I, for one, don't want to. And I feel at peace—unforgiving heart and all.

Dear Kristen and Jolenta,

But when you don't forgive, you're really only punishing yourself! I beg you both, please forgive for your own sake!

—RH

Dear RH,

I'm sorry, but I think I disagree with you. I've tried the pure forgiveness route. And it has worked with small things. Mostly it works well with people I trust. That core group that I know have my back no matter what because our relationship is based on a solid foundation of love and honest communication. But this doesn't work when I truly think someone has hurt me with malicious or blindly selfish intent, and especially if that's the only side of them that they've chosen to share with me.

Perhaps I'm not as generous as you when it comes to giving perpetrators the benefit of the doubt. But I have found that voicing my story, defining it in my terms, identifying how I was hurt by a person or situation, and being as specific as possible are what have helped me work through the often-punishing feelings that resentment leads to.

For me, finding my voice and using it to retell my version of events and explore how I've held on to this pain causing myself years of residual damage is way more healing than feeling obligated to "play nice" when it's not in my heart to do so.

—Jolenta

AIM TO HAVE IT ALL

Jolenta

The most basic thing about me is definitely my wedding. On paper, it's the one time in my life I appeared to "have it all." But I assure you I did not have it all, because having it all isn't real!

My wedding truly did look like a magical hipster bullshit fairy tale brought to life. It was so idyllic it was like Pinterest became a sentient monster and walked the earth. It stomped around barking orders like

"Succulents must be in all the bouquets!"

"All the groomsmen will wear leather suspenders so they look old-timey!"

And my personal favorite, "The ring bearer shall be the bride's senile childhood dog!"

On the outside I was killing it. I was a wedding planning beast. But I was conflicted. The deeper I got into planning my wedding, the more grossed out I became by the whole wedding industry. It's an insult to women, a hugely lucrative scheme to capitalize on the idea that you finally found someone to love you. I found it hard to be a passionate feminist and still care about how the wood grain on the tree stump candleholders looked.

And it's superhard to be a feminist and also ask your parents to spend thousands of dollars so you can publicly declare the fact that you're going to try your hardest to bone only one person for the rest of your life. But I wanted to have it all, and that meant making this promise to bone this one guy forever while dressed like a pretty, pretty princess.

Do you guys know how hard it is to become a dang princess? *So hard.* And not very feminist-feeling at all. I demeaned myself on the regular to become a princess. I stood naked on a tarp in a woman's basement while I paid her to airbrush a tan onto every inch of my skin. I sat for two hours while a woman taped my eyes shut and glued fake eyelashes one by one to my face. And on top of all that I'd forced myself to give up carbs for six months.

This was a big mistake. My stomach was like, "What are you doing to me? I don't know who I am without carbs! I shall curse you with constant diarrhea!"

Seriously, if you Google "carb-free living" plus "diarrhea," you'll find many a forum post that says, "Oh yeah, it's totally normal." On an intellectual level I knew this could not be right. Eating healthy should not turn your poo liquid.

But I was determined to have it all on my wedding day. And if barfing out of my ass was the only way to do that, then *so be it.* Because I'm a *feminist,* and feminists deserve to have it all even if having it all is often defined by outdated sexist and classist ideals! You see why I was so conflicted? This kind of stuff is hard to reconcile.

Part of the reason I was determined to have a blog-worthy wedding was that Brad and I do not have a fairy-tale story. We were messy. We were on-and-off friends with benefits for a year. And after we started dating, our love was still sloppy.

How sloppy? Well, one evening over a quiet dinner at home during our engagement I noticed a big ol' blackhead just begging to be squeezed. I'm obsessed with picking zits and blackheads, so needless to say, I very much wanted at that bad boy on Brad's neck. *I must make it mine.* But this blackhead was off-limits. I wasn't allowed to pick anything on him, because according to him it hurts and feels "disrespectful." But I wanted this blackhead bad. It was a perfect specimen, the nice big kind that can easily be mistaken for a freckle. I knew it was going to be so satisfying to pop.

So I asked real nice, "Hey, buddy, you got a real bad blackhead on your neck—how 'bout I do you a favor and get rid of it for you?"

"No," he dryly responded.

"I'll do the dishes if you let me." I was starting to get desperate now and offered to do the chores he normally took care of.

"No," he said again without looking up from his dinner.

"I'll do the laundry?"

"Still *no.*"

I decided to go all in with my final offer: "I'll suck your dick."

And with that, Brad silently stopped eating his meal and slowly leaned his head forward to present his neck. I went to *town* on his blackhead, and it popped like a dream. And the second I was done with my pop, Brad sat up straight and whipped his junk out at the table. And I followed through on my end of the bargain, because I'm a woman of my word.

Now you're probably thinking, *Jolenta, you're disgusting. Why are you telling me this?* You're right—*I am gross*—just as gross as my fiancé. Together we are two gross garbage people who trade popped blackheads for a blow job. *That* is the kind of messy lovebirds we were mere months before we said our vows. No wonder I felt like my ethereal, Lauren Conrad wanna-be, woodland-themed hipster nuptials and my pretty "princess bod" were a veil of lies draped over the pell-mell, uncensored vibe of myself and my relationship.

My picture-perfect wedding was fueled by Pinterest standards and diarrhea. It was gorgeous, but it just didn't feel like it really represented who we were. And because of that, the day felt a bit more hollow and a smidge less special than I expected.

My wedding story illustrates a greater theory I'm forming about the idea of "having it all." I'm learning that appearing to have it all externally is nothing compared to fulfilling your actual dreams. Thus any book laying out concrete directions on how to have it all is probably full of hot air.

There are lots of books out there like this. Kristen and I have lived by plenty of them, and they've all left us feeling unsatisfied and inadequate. In *Girl, Wash Your Face*, Rachel Hollis implies that having it all is defined by working with rich people, having enough money for designer purses, and living in a stereotypical straight family unit with a gaggle of kids by the time you're thirty. This very basic ideology led to frustratingly simple advice to live by for Kristen and me. But instead of feeling empowered, I felt bummed out, because I was living by advice that was just another reminder of the fact that my goals don't always match up with society's expectations of me.

Randi Zuckerberg's book *Pick Three* was another we lived by that was centered on the idea of having it all. Randi, the older sister of Mark Zuckerberg, is a Harvard graduate. She worked as the director of communications at Facebook, started her own media company, started a family, wrote a book, and even starred in a Broadway musical.

In her book, Zuckerberg describes how one of the hardest moments of her life, getting into Harvard as a drama nerd and not a more well-rounded student, taught her that having lopsided priorities can help you appear to have it all. Relatable, right?

Zuckerberg believes she's so successful because she's still using that lopsided focus of hers. Rather than trying to do it all every day, she chooses only three areas in her life to focus on and do to the best of her abilities. That way she can "have it all (just not every day)."

Living by this advice drove Kristen and me nuts. Kristen was especially bothered by the way Zuckerberg advises readers to categorize the people in their lives into friends and family, then says you should choose strategically who to make time for. Kristen considers her friends to be family, and so do I. How were we supposed to break them up into a sort of A team and B team?

Kristen also really struggled with how Randi made sleep a category, and it was one of the things she would choose from every day when she picked her three things to focus on. Think about this. She's definitely not picking sleep every day if it's one of many rotating choices, is she? *What?* Sleep is a priority only a few times a week? How is that cool or healthy? Kristen would posit that it is neither.

There was no room for spontaneity when we lived by *Pick Three,* and that was a big issue for both Kristen and myself. Every task we took on was related to making it look like we "had it all." But it turned out we didn't want the "all" we were being instructed to strive for.

I don't know about you, but I don't have to want a name-brand job. I don't need four kids before I turn thirty-three to be a success. And I was disheartened to learn how many advice books push women to accept the burden of finding the balance between appearing to be 100 percent devoted to family and 100 percent devoted to career at the same time. This is an impossible task!

I wish more books would talk about how the notion of having it all keeps women down and saddles us with double the expectations and obligations of those who aren't determined to "have it all." Implementing endless life hacks that give the illusion of balance will never ease the dissatisfaction that comes from being in a system rigged against you.

Doing it all, having it all, being a pretty pretty princess on your wedding day—the more I explore these vague goals, the more I feel they exist to distract those of us who can't afford to pay to "have it all" by advising us to live up to impossible standards that we'll never meet. Any book that idealizes this trap can go bye-bye, as far as I'm concerned. So if you ever come across advice like this in your reading adventures, feel free to put that book down. Your energy is far better spent figuring out what "all" means to you than aiming to be what someone else's basic-ass version of "having it all" should look like.

Dear Kristen and Jolenta,

I'm not saying anyone else should aim to have it all, but I personally want to! I want the loving spouse and adorable kids and fulfilling job and supportive friends and nice house and smoking-hot body. What's so wrong with wanting it all?

—GM

Dear GM,

Feel free to aim for what you want. We're not going to stop you! But we also don't want you to feel as though it's your fault if you never get it all, or if you get it only after decades of toil and setbacks.

The fact is, fulfilling careers don't usually happen overnight. Likewise with loving relationships and supportive friendships. These all take time, effort, sacrifices, and their fair share of frustrations.

As for the other items on your list, these require money. Nice houses cost money. The clothing and feeding of adorable children costs money. Child care costs money if you want to continue working in that fulfilling career.

But let's say, despite the obstacles, you really do manage to get it all. If you do, congratulations! You're living your dream! We just ask you one favor: Please don't look down at all the other people who haven't achieved what you have. Very few people, outside the well-to-do and well connected, get all they want in the time frame in which they want it. And it may also be the case that all those other people who haven't achieved what you have actually never wanted to. There's a good chance they had different dreams than you.

—Kristen

P.S. We don't even know what you mean by "smoking-hot body," but trust us when we say all bodies are beautiful, including yours when you're feeling neither smoking nor hot.

THE LAW OF ATTRACTION

Kristen

Once upon a time there was a little boy who dreamed of becoming an astronaut. In all his spare time, the boy shot off bottle rockets and drew pictures of space shuttles and built model airplanes. He read books about space exploration and watched movies that took place on other planets. And with his friends, he'd play games that took place in an imaginary version of the outer limits.

As the boy grew older, he took classes in aeronautics and physics. He visited air and space museums. He conducted his own science experiments at home and in the classroom. He even learned to fly a plane.

And throughout his life, from the time he was four years old, this boy would dedicate large portions of his mental energy to his space fantasies. He daydreamed about life on other planets. He fell asleep picturing himself exploring those planets. And he talked to all who would listen about his hopes of spending time in outer space.

Day after day and year after year, both this boy's heart and his actions were committed to his astronaut dreams.

Surely there was no other child as dedicated to the idea of space travel as this boy was.

And, friends, you will likely not be surprised in the slightest to learn the outcome of this story: The young boy who dreamed all his life of going to space eventually grew up to program computers. That boy is my husband. He loves his work and his life. And no, he is not an astronaut.

Now, the Law of Attraction (which I'm capitalizing only for the sake of believers who always treat it like an official thing) would dictate that my husband absolutely should be an astronaut at this point in his life. According to its logic, thoughts inevitably become things. In the simplest of terms: Think a good thing and it will come true. Think a bad thing and it will also come true.

The wordier explanation of the Law of Attraction goes something like this: (1) People and their thoughts are made from energy. (2) Like energies attract like energies. (3) Thus, if you put out negative thoughts into the universe, you'll attract negative things. Likewise, if you put out positive thoughts into the universe, you will attract positive things.

So, if you think you can be rich, you will be rich. If you think your cancer will disappear, it will. If you think you can be a TV star, have a bodacious booty, and be wildly famous, you will become Kim Kardashian.

On the flip side, if you are poor, the Law of Attraction dictates that you brought your poverty on yourself by thinking poor thoughts. If you have cancer, it's because you attracted cancer to yourself with your cancerous mind-set. And if your grandpa died in the Holocaust, he was asking for it with his negative energy.

Obviously, Jolenta and I, being mostly logical people, consider this "law" a load of hogwash. First and foremost, it assumes that people and their individual thoughts exist in vacuums. But if this is the case, why are black men twenty-one times more likely to be victims of police violence in the United States than white men? Is this because all black men are coincidentally all thinking at the same time, *I really want and deserve to be beaten up by cops*? More likely, it's because we live in a nation with a four-hundred-year history of slavery, Jim Crow laws, unwarranted mass incarceration, institutionalized racism, legal segregation, and negative depictions of black men in the media.

To take things in the opposite direction, let's look at all the filthy rich white men in America who hold most of our public offices and corporate leadership positions. Did all of these men reach their positions of power because—by coincidence—they all just happened to be visualizing money and power at the same time and with more intensity than anyone else for the past four hundred years? More likely, it's because these men benefited from generational wealth, social capital, and all the same systems that hurt the black men I just mentioned.

Nonetheless, a number of self-help books claim that the Law of Attraction is as real as the law of gravity. Author after author—from Jen Sincero of *You Are a Badass* to Rhonda

Byrne of *The Secret*—insists that their own accomplishments in life come down to their wealth-generating and health-attracting thoughts.

Now, to be clear, I think it's great to have uplifting thoughts. When things aren't going my way, I try to remind myself that I still have a lot to be thankful for. Jolenta spins her bad moments into funny stories that fill the world with laughter. We both do our best to tap into our optimism.

But have my happy thoughts stopped me from having ill health and job losses? Have Jolenta's funny stories prevented her from being sexually harassed? Have they prevented those nearest and dearest to me from dying too young? No, plenty of lousy things have happened to Jolenta and me, despite my happy mind-set and her awesome storytelling.

The fact is: The Law of Attraction is a bunch of hooey.

And yet, it's something we hear about again and again in self-help books, in pop culture, and in the memoirs of rich, successful people. Of course it is. That's because, for those who've made it to the top (including bestselling self-help authors), the Law of Attraction provides reassurances that the top is where they deserve to be. It creates a framework for the universe in which winners can say, "I won because I had the winningest attitude." It allows people who have the most advantages in life to completely ignore their advantages and instead believe everything they have came to them because of the force of their own will. And it gives successful people permission to blame those who are less successful in life for their failings.

In so many ways, the world would be a fantastic place if the Law of Attraction were true. Innocent children wouldn't be dying in famines. Jolenta and I would have zero experiences with smarmy men. My husband would be an astronaut.

But it's not. And as long as people continue to pin all their hopes on this fake "law," they'll also be giving themselves permission to ignore both the real ways that bad things are consistently allowed to happen and the hard work that must be done for good things to be more equitably distributed.

Dear Kristen and Jolenta,

Let's be real. The Law of Attraction is just a rebranding of the Power of Positive Thinking. And that's not a bad thing! I think life is better when we think positively! Isn't positivity what you're always lauding when you talk about gratitude and positive self-talk?

—CF

Dear CF,

Positivity rocks! It's the best. I highly recommend positive self-talk, finding gratitude, and spreading the love. But here's my question: How is declaring the benefit of looking on the bright side a "scientific law" the same thing as positivity? Believing there is a supernatural law akin to gravity that can help me manifest money with my thoughts and blames me if I get sick (because I must have been sending bad vibes out into the universe) is not at all like trying to have a positive outlook, right?

—Jolenta

PART 3

8

Things We Wish More Books Recommended

STOP COMPARING YOURSELF TO OTHERS

Kristen

Back when I was a wee lass in the single digits, I remember playing beauty shop with some of the other little girls in my neighborhood. We brushed bright pink blush across our cheeks and agreed that we all looked magnificent. We applied shimmery lipstick to our little mouths. Beautiful! And then it came time for the vibrant blue eye shadow we'd all been excited about. We took turns applying it and then, looking around at one another, my little white friends asked why the shadow looked so weird on my sister and me. Notably, both my sister and I are Asian.

Now, let me make clear: I think there's nothing wrong with noticing the ways that we're different. I love that we're all different! And pretending not to see our differences, claiming to be color-blind, exclaiming "There's only one race, the human race!"—all these things do more to erase than to honor our uniqueness.

That being said, pointing out that a difference is "weird"

can feel like a real bummer to a kid (or an adult, for that matter). It takes a difference and applies a good-bad value to it, when in fact there's no such thing as an inherently good or bad physical trait—only subjective societal values projected on those traits based on the trends and times.

But of course my little white friends, with their limited vocabularies and limited worldviews, simply saw our differences as weird. And how could they not? After all, almost every aspect of our culture—from our illustrated children's books to the actors we saw on television to the models on the covers of the magazines at the grocery store to the packages of our prepared foods—presented a single image of what was "normal" and what was "beautiful," and that was a white woman with a folded upper eyelid, as opposed to an Asian woman with no eyelid fold at all.

Immersed in our homogeneous white culture, it was almost inevitable that at their tender ages, our little friends would see my sister and me as weird. And suddenly, I did, too. Occasionally, and then more and more frequently, I began comparing my physicality to others around me, always placing my differences in the bad category. I noticed I had a very long torso and short, muscular legs, while all my white friends seemed to have the opposite proportions. I noticed that clothes didn't fit me the way they fit my white friends. I noticed that my skin was darker than that of almost everyone else I knew.

Of course, the agony that comes from comparison isn't just about race. Jolenta—who is white—felt it very deeply herself growing up. For most of her childhood, she was painfully aware of the fact that she was the least affluent person in a very affluent school. She was almost always the tallest, biggest, and bustiest girl in a sea of Waspy, button-nosed pixies. She couldn't wear the same clothes as her female classmates without being called "inappropriate" by her disgusting PE teacher.

Getting out of the compare and despair mind-set is hard—especially when we're taught it at such a young age. And frankly, I can't think of a single self-help book we've lived by that's deeply and thoroughly explained why we should. If anything, they've indirectly and sometimes directly suggested that comparison is the ticket to a better life. For example, in *You Are a Badass,* Jen Sincero suggests we surround ourselves with people who are more successful than we are—with the understanding that their greatness will rub off on us. But in order to do that, we obviously must first compare ourselves to everyone around us and ask—Who's doing better than I am? Who's doing worse? How do they all compare to one another? How do I compare to them?

There are flaws in this kind of thinking. Among these flaws: the presumption that there's a single definition of more versus less (and by extension, good versus bad, rich versus poor, successful versus failing, and so on). But that's simply not true.

For me, a dream life centers on lots of fantastic friends, plenty of great adventures, my dear husband, and storytelling in some form or another. For Jolenta, the dream life includes many of these same things, but also her dog, Frank; her husband (not mine); and plenty of downtime in her cozy Brooklyn apartment. Meanwhile, mainstream entertainment is trying to sell us McMansions, giant lawns, sports cars, Ivy League degrees, expensive jewelry, and two point five children. Anyone playing the old comparison game might conclude that my dream life and Jolenta's life are worse than the McMansion life. But we know they're not. Screw comparison, if that's what comparison's verdict is going to be!

And let's be real: Our comparison methods tend to be faulty. Appearances can be deceiving, and even if people look like they have the life we want, they don't necessarily. And even if they do, it's possible they went through horrible things to get it. Alternatively, they may have had it all handed to them. Regardless, they didn't have to live my life, and if they did, would they be where they are? I'm guessing not. I'm also guessing that plenty of people with "dream lives" aren't happy all the time. Even "beautiful" people feel bad about themselves sometimes. And plenty of people who look like they have it all go home to cheating spouses, debt collectors, and a sense of hopelessness about where their lives are going. As my friends in the AA community say, "Don't compare your insides to other people's outsides." Add to that Sophia Amoruso's mantra, "Don't compare your hustle to their highlight reel" (an especially useful thing to remember if you're someone who tends to take Instagram and Facebook feeds at face value).

Personally, I'm happiest when I'm not comparing myself to others. As Teddy Roosevelt famously said, "Comparison is the thief of joy." Why rob myself of joy? Why not instead embrace and revel in all the uniquely good things in my life? And when unhappiness strikes, as it inevitably will from time to time, why not focus on how to help myself, rather than go down a "woe is me" rabbit hole of comparing myself to others? Isn't it better to see a therapist, talk with friends, go on a walk, map out a list of places I'd like to visit, read a good book, or do something else constructive? Anything is better than comparing and despairing.

Of course, saying "Don't compare yourself to others" is easier than doing it. And all the logic and all the action in the world can sometimes still not be enough to pull us out of the throes of comparison. And when that happens to me, I have one last weapon I enlist: I take a moment to think back to little me, and all the other small children in the world who are being told they look weird or abnormal in that blue eye shadow (or striped swimsuit or "flesh-colored" Band-Aid or what have you). I think back to teen Jolenta, being told her clothes were inappropriate because her body didn't fit a certain teacher's ideal. I think of all the good-bad binaries our younger selves were fed—binaries that placed thin, rich, white people on one side and fat, brown, poor people on the other. And then I cut it out.

I'm a good person. And I know you are, too. We don't need to compare ourselves to anyone. We are all beautiful and worthy of love as we are.

Dear Kristen and Jolenta,

Do you hate straight white men? With some regularity, you mention how easy straight white men have it. We don't all have it easy! I grew up in a blue-collar family. And not all the world's problems are my fault.
—AZ

Dear AZ,

We don't hate all straight men. We're actually both married to straight white men, it's wild. But we do hate straight white men who write books telling women and minorities to live their lives as though they also have it just as easy as straight white men.

Annoyingly, many self-help authors are white, male, and heterosexual. And often they write as though everyone experiences the world the way they do—from the top of the societal power structure. As long as authors account for societal inequities and acknowledge that sexism and racism and other concepts that promote inequality are actual forces in the world that no amount of solo, early morning gratitude journaling can dismantle, we're cool with anyone. We're not cool with the ones who don't account for walks of life they can't relate to, and most of those are dudes of the straight and white variety.
—Jolenta

CHECK IN WITH YOUR FEELINGS

Jolenta

I have a secret to tell you guys—acting schools are nuts.

Seriously, they have a very cultlike vibe. They tell you that everything you think and believe is a lie, they break you down, and they rebuild you using their logic and teachings. On top of that, they really stress the fact that you have no time for your family or friends anymore because you are following the true way—you are pursuing art. So, um . . . that's pretty culty.

In 2008 I was fresh out of university, and instead of entering the workforce during the second coming of the Great Depression, I took the little savings I had that wasn't lost in the stock market and moved from San Francisco to New York to go to a conservatory acting program. I was a perfect candidate for acting school. I loved theater, had no real acting technique, and had no idea who I was.

These qualities left me vulnerable and desperate for guidance. I was just a lost little girl who wanted to spend her last few dimes on a place to call my own where someone would tell me how to think. So when I found myself in New York at a slightly prestigious acting conservatory, I was totally ready to have my brain washed. Lucky for me I was about to be brainwashed with some very good advice.

The best part of acting school, and the most effective brainwashing tool, was the feedback—basically all we did was rehearse scenes, perform them for our classmates and instructors, and then get ripped apart by critiques from everyone. The feedback started simple. After my first scene I was told by my instructor, "Your posture is horrible," and a classmate chimed in to add, "She must have really low self-esteem because she won't root herself to the ground."

For two years, the feedback I received was basically the same—I'm not owning my space, I'm not rooted to the earth (still don't know what that means), I'm not harnessing my power. I roughly translated this to "You're a rootless bitch who hates yourself, and you can't even cry." Crying is incredibly important in acting school. Everyone who has ever been to acting school will say it's *not* about learning how to cry, but this is a lie. You are basically a failure unless you can start crying at the drop of a hat.

After a lifetime of undiagnosed ADHD, which often led to emotional outbursts, and a childhood spent with a father who has trouble with empathy, I had learned how to do what I call locking it down. Because my emotions were so big and so often misunderstood, I spent a lot of time getting in trouble for reacting emotionally. So instead of checking in with how I felt whenever anything went down, I tried to simply dismiss or ignore my feelings. I'd squelch my feelings and tell myself I was being irrational.

Locking it down is a great defense mechanism, but it leaves you tearless—and to be a full, card-carrying member of the cult that is acting school, I *had* to cry.

One day I was in the respite that was voice class, and all it asked of me was to do yoga poses and work on breathing. (And yes, people often cry in voice class, but it's not required; you aren't a failure if you don't cry.)

In this class we were doing Fitzmaurice work, which requires you to train your body to sort of tremble while you do different yoga poses until your body is shaking and convulsing as though you are having a very intense orgasm. While your body is doing all this, your breath is supposed to fully release, or something like that.

While in this class, I was in a position known as camel doing my thing and my voice instructor came over. She's a fabulous former dancer who has an edgy zen vibe, and she was coaching me. This simply means she asked to touch me in various places to help me "release" my voice and said things like "Breathe into your knees, breathe into your shoulder," and so on.

When she got to my sternum and lightly touched it, something strange happened. It felt like a hot ball of molten lava had formed in my chest, exploded, and sent a wave of searing magma through my body, and I started to cry.

Once I started crying I couldn't stop. I cried all the time. I cried when I ate, I cried when I was in the shower, I'd cry as I fell asleep.

As I cried, memories flashed through my mind. Every time I felt ashamed for being "too sensitive," every time my heart had been broken, every loss, every time I self-destructed. I cried all the tears I had tried to lock away. It took weeks to stop crying; I had a lot to make up for, apparently.

When I was finally done, I felt like a new woman. I was lighter and brighter, I stood up taller, and I became a much better actor and human being in general. Once I got in touch with where I had been hiding my emotions, I could finally access them, check in with them, and communicate them to others!

I'm forever grateful for that day in voice class and the ridiculous, shaky yoga pose that helped me find my feelings again. Turns out feelings are superimportant; they're like a barometer for how well a situation is meeting our needs. When our feelings barometer starts to beep (is that what barometers do?), we get to pause and figure out what we want to better have our needs met. What's not to like about feelings!?

So many books Kristen and I have lived by paint a picture of the optimal human as someone who has the ability to choose positive feelings over those yucky ones, with the end goal being a life that appears to be free from negative emotions. That book I mentioned earlier that tells readers to admit they're liars, *The Subtle Art of Not Giving a F*ck*, is a perfect example of this. In his book, Mark Manson says the first step toward living your best life is to take responsibility for everything that occurs in your life, regardless of who is actually at fault.

The book says we should do this because even though plenty of things are beyond our control, we can always control how we react and read into them. This is a great idea in theory, but hard to actually implement considering emotions are natural and very hard-to-control human reactions that we use to communicate with others and ourselves. So overriding your feelings or negating them seems kind of counterproductive, right? It was for Kristen and me; we found it to be frustrating and in no way life enhancing to try to gaslight ourselves.

Most of the books we've encountered while living by the book do not touch on the fact that you have to check in with your emotions to even know if you're happy, and learn what bums you out. Why on earth would you try to push these natural and helpful indicators away?

I don't think it really matters how you get at your emotions as long as you find a way to listen to them and let them run their course. For me, it was that voice class and doing orgasm-mimicking Fitzmaurice work. I hope that for you it doesn't have to be such a production, but even if it does, who will really care?

Over the past few years I've learned that the less energy I waste on trying to change my natural emotional responses to the things life throws at me, the more content I am. And as a bonus, I have more energy left to get myself through emotional situations using less wacky means, such as watching the birds outside my window and speed-walking through Manhattan. There are so many great ways to check in with yourself and honor your emotions, like crafting or swimming or even therapy! I'd rather try that stuff than attempt to convince myself my feelings aren't real and end up crying for two weeks straight after an ex–modern dancer touched my sternum again.

DO THINGS
IN CHUNKS

Kristen

I have a confession: I am a world-class procrastinator. From the time I was in middle school until right this very minute, I've always put things off, pushed things back, and found excuses to do just about anything other than the task at hand.

Is a script due tomorrow? In that case, I'll spend today trying on all my spring dresses to see which ones still fit from last year. Do I have a meeting to prepare for this afternoon? If so, I'll spend the next hour "working" on my social media. And don't get me started on an arbitrary giant project that must be completed from home. I'll spend all day watching reruns of *Little House on the Prairie* and eating corn chips until I'm forced to stay up all night working on it.

This isn't to say that I don't meet my deadlines. I always do. And often, my work is good enough for me to be proud of. Sometimes it even wins awards. But I know for a fact that I wouldn't get things done—at the last minute or otherwise—without a few strategies.

First and foremost, I think about those who are counting on me and who will be let down if I don't pull my weight and complete my tasks. Being accountable (and filled with guilt) helps me get things done. Second, I remind myself that done is better than perfect. Knowing that I don't have to write a Nobel-worthy invoice or the best memo of all time keeps me from perfectionist-driven procrastination. But of course both these strategies are more about mind-set than about action. When it comes to action, I have one big rule: Stop looking at the big picture and instead do things in chunks.

Now, I know this is contrary to what a lot of self-help books say. Most books Jolenta and I have lived by have encouraged us to look at the big picture, keep our eyes on the prize, consider the whole rather than the parts, focus on our long-term goals, or draw up a ten-year plan. These books argue that considering the whole will keep us motivated and looking at the big picture will keep things in perspective. But when it comes to the day-to-day aspects of life and to getting things done, this advice has done more to paralyze me than motivate me. Chunking does the opposite. And I have dozens of ways to do it.

One way I chunk tasks is by setting a time limit. I'll say to myself, for example: *You only have to fold laundry for three minutes. You don't have to commit to doing it forever.* More often than not, I'll find that once I get over the hurdle of sitting down with the laundry, I'll fold for longer than three minutes. Usually I'll fold the whole basket; inertia takes over. But even if it doesn't, I'll know I did more than

I would have if I hadn't set that three-minute time limit in the first place.

Getting Things Done, by David Allen, is one of the few books we've come across that has a similar strategy. It's called the two-minute rule, and it works like this: Any tasks that come your way that will take less than two minutes to complete should be done immediately. Don't put them on a to-do list. Don't put them off till tomorrow. Do them now.

Note: The time-limit strategy doesn't work just for job- and chore-related tasks. I also use this strategy when I'm entering new social situations, such as going to a party where I barely know anyone, or attending an event with new coworkers, or going on Internet dates (back in my single days). I call it my seventy-five-minute rule, and it's based on the idea that staying at an event for an hour is polite, but staying for just over an hour is better, because it looks less obviously like a time limit. In my experience, seventy-five minutes is enough time to have fun and get out of my shell, and also not so much time that it's terrifying. Since we've become friends, Jolenta has also begun to adopt this rule. She's told me that it might be the best idea I've ever come up with.

Another situation that chunking is especially useful in is the one I'm in the middle of now: writing a book. Being able to write a two-hundred-page book for a respected publishing house is a huge honor. But it's also an overwhelming task. Thinking of the enormity of it just makes me want to crawl under the covers for the rest of the year and watch Laura Ingalls Wilder go fishing. But taken in chunks, it becomes more manageable.

I learned this firsthand when I wrote my last book, *So You Want to Start a Podcast*. The book is a how-to guide, but it's also a thinly veiled manifesto about the power of individual voices and why stories matter. How would I blend all this into one cohesive book of more than two hundred pages? The big picture was terrifying.

First, I enlisted that mental trick of accountability (to my agent, to my editor, to anyone I could think of who was counting on me). Second, I reminded myself of my other mental mantra: that done is better than perfect. Even if I just wrote stream of consciousness nonsense, it was better than writing nothing at all. Then, I moved along to actively chunking.

I started with a method of chunking I haven't mentioned yet: doing the easiest or funnest part first. Jolenta is a pro at this. And I like to think I'm pretty good at it as well. For example, when I cut my fingernails (a task I abhor because my nails seemingly grow an inch every night as I sleep), I always cut the left-hand nails first, because it's easier for me to maneuver the clippers with my right hand, being right-handed and all. I then move on to the less fun task of maneuvering the nail clippers with my south paw.

In the case of my podcasting book, writing a love letter to my readers seemed like the easiest and funnest way to start. Telling people I adore them comes easy for me. Reminding people that they are unique and beautiful and worthy fills my heart with joy. Cheering is one of my favorite things ever. And so, I sat down and wrote about how I believed in everyone taking the time to read my book. I told them they had it in them to tell great stories. And I assured them that I'd give them the tools they needed to share their voices in the ways they wanted to. In addition to being fun to write, my love letter set the tone for what my book was: *both* a step-by-step guide *and* the cheering squad I believe everyone deserves. That love letter became my book's introduction.

After that, I jotted down all the steps that I felt were required to make, distribute, and promote a podcast. After I'd deleted some and added others, there were thirty-seven steps in total. And then I organized all the steps under seven specific headings: Dream It, Write It, Host It, Cast It, Make It, Share It, and Grow It.

From there, the book screamed, "Write me in chunks! I'm already broken down that way!" And, fortunately, the chunks were manageable. With thirty-seven steps, and two hundred pages to fill, each chapter had to average out to only about five or six pages. Could I explain each step in about six pages? I thought so, and so that's what I set out to do. Each day, I woke up and said, "You only have to write one step. If you write more than that, terrific. If you write less than that, at least you have more on paper than you did yesterday."

Some days I wrote only a few sentences. Other days I wrote three chapters. And a lot of the time, I'd manage to write only by combining the chapter-chunking strategy with other chunking techniques. For example, if I wasn't enjoying the chapter at hand, I'd jump ahead to a chapter I knew would be more fun to write (chunking for fun!). Or, when the idea of writing for a whole day seemed too torturous to even consider, I'd tell myself, *You only have to write for two and a half hours* (chunking with a time limit!).

It wasn't always easy. And it wasn't always fun. But when all was said and done, that chunking helped me complete my first draft in only two months.

Another chunking technique I haven't mentioned yet—one that may be the easiest to start with—is to-do lists. I keep a running to-do list on my computer that I add to, rearrange, and cross things off of every day. (Jolenta keeps a bullet journal that's almost the same in terms of purpose, but much prettier.) The items on my list include all my freelance duties, chores, errands, appointments, social engagements, emails I need to send, and people I need to call. Some of the items are small, like "Text Amir to ask if he wants to have lunch next week." Some are bigger, like "Write the next script." But no matter what, I make sure I cross multiple things off daily. Doing that gives me a sense of accomplishment.

In addition to working well with chores and work-related tasks, Jolenta and I have both found that to-do-list chunking helps when we're going through a bout of the blues. Like most people, we've lost jobs and gone through breakups and dealt with tough transitions, and sometimes we're just sad for reasons we can't put our fingers on. At times like these, walking through the world as a fully functioning adult can feel impossible. And so, rather than focus on the amorphous and overwhelming work of adulthood, Jolenta and I break all the tasks of daily living into tiny chunks. "Kristen, get out of bed. Well done, Kristen!" "Jolenta, walk to the bathroom and splash water on your face. You did it!" "Kristen, put on clothes. Nice." "Jolenta, walk out the door. You've got this."

Of course, chunking isn't perfect. As I said, even when I'm doing my best to enlist it, I sometimes don't accomplish as much as I'd like. And in some cases, it's hard to know how to break work or life down into chunks. For example, when your job is made up of a never-ending stream of re-dundant labor—like fast-food service or cashiering—the only chunks you can really create are around break times or the hours on the clock. And even then, the work just has to get done, or you'll be fired.

Likewise with doing the emotional work of fixing a mar-riage. Or caring for people who can't care for themselves. Or healing your psychological wounds when you've grown up in an abusive household.

So, chunking isn't a cure-all. Life has a lot of hard parts that can't be compartmentalized or broken down. Some things just have to be done slow and steady all the time, or ignored for a while and then done all at once.

But when it comes to more concrete and distinct tasks— from the stuff of housekeeping to the steps required to get out the front door in the morning—I find that chunking helps. In some cases, it makes things more fun. And above all, chunking keeps me from being so overwhelmed by all the things I can't do that it's hard to focus on all the things I can.

The fact is, I can't write more than two hundred pages in a single sitting. I can't deep-clean my whole home in one day. And I can't transform my entire body into a temple of hygiene all at once. But I can write a love letter. I can fold socks for three minutes. I can clip the nails on my left hand.

And sometimes, that's enough. After many days or months, it might even add up to a complete and whole big picture.

MAKE FRIENDS
WITH YOUR BODY

Jolenta

Did you know that back in the 1400s sailors who started seeing manatees in tropical waters thought they'd spotted mermaids?

I think about this fact all the time. Not because it's a funny anecdote from history but because it's such a glaring example of how our beauty standards have changed through time. An animal we have nicknamed the "sea cow" used to be mistaken for a majestic aquatic maiden. Imagine, what if the Little Mermaid we grew up with looked like a frickin' manatee? We'd all feel great about our bodies and our inability to magically and attractively flip soaking wet hair (which is impossible).

I never thought about my body much until I turned fifteen and grew boobs basically overnight. I went from mosquito bites to bigger than double Ds in what seemed like twenty-four hours!

While this may sound cool, let me remind you that naturally large breasts are *very* different from man-made large breasts. Real big tits are heavy and painful and turn into giant flat pancakes when you lie on your back. They aren't fun when you're fifteen, or at least they weren't for me. There were so many downsides that it was hard to decide which I hated most. There was the physical pain in my shoulders and back that came with carrying around my new figure. There was the difficulty shopping, because nothing was made to fit people as busty as I was. And of course there was unwanted male attention of all kinds, from strangers to my overly handsy and demeaning PE teacher.

After puberty hit, I was forced to navigate the world as an adult woman, because that's what I looked like to everyone who didn't know I couldn't legally drive yet. All of this because my body randomly chose to grow big boobs! I felt like my boobs were profoundly unfair. I didn't choose to become an object of desire. I didn't mean to grow into a body that implied I was mature or ready for sex. And I certainly didn't mean to be in a body that, once it blossomed, seemed to become a blank canvas inviting any sort of projection a man felt like seeing when he looked at me.

To take back some ownership of this rogue body of mine, I tried to embrace my new figure. I went out and bought something to really express myself. And like any good teenager in the year 2000, I went to the Gap to do that. I picked out a modest light yellow halter top, with a thick strap, high neck, and built-in bralette. It was perfect—not too much cleavage, in a color that looked great on me—and I couldn't wait to wear it.

On the first beautiful spring day of the year, I finally got a chance to debut my new top. And as I ate lunch that day, minding my own business and listening to my Discman, I saw my PE teacher. This is a man who had many opinions about my body. He loved to tell me I was overweight, never going to date, and all about how he was going to "help" me become desirable, all while touching me too much. So needless to say I wasn't happy when I saw him pointing and looking at me from across the room as he talked to my math teacher. Before I knew it, my math teacher was rushing toward me.

"Jolenta," he said. "You have to cover up right now, that shirt is totally inappropriate for school."

My heart sank. I apologized and started putting on my sweater while a wave of searing hot shame swept through my body. I had no idea I looked so horrible. But then, as I watched him walk away, something bizarre happened. On his way out, he passed a classmate of mine, Emily. Emily was tiny and skinny and maybe wore an A-cup, if anything. And *get this*—she was wearing the same top as I was in the exact same color!

And what did he do when he passed this perfect specimen of teen womanhood? He walked past her and didn't bat an eye. Didn't say a thing to her about being inappropriate or covering up. He didn't even seem to notice her.

That day it became abundantly clear to me that it wasn't my top that was offending this grown man in charge of my education. It was me. Me and my horrible huge monster tits made a dude pushing forty with a daughter of his own so uncomfortable that he had to tell me about it.

It wasn't until the #MeToo movement finally caught fire

after Donald Trump was elected in 2016 that I even began to consider that I hadn't deserved the demeaning treatment I received. I thought I was supposed to pretend that all the degrading and annoying things women put up with because they are in bodies that slightly differ from those of their male counterparts were all in my head, or par for the course. And often self-help books are part of the problem.

The majority of the self-help books out there don't encourage us to examine the damage done by the societal standards placed upon those who identify as female. The vast majority of books we've lived by don't even want us to be friends with our bodies. They veil fat shaming and unachievable standards of beauty as health and a way of life. When this way of life proves to be ultimately unsustainable (see Kristen's chapter on diets for more about this), we spiral back into the same shame and despair that prompted us to seek out self-help and the whole cycle repeats itself. This sounds counterproductive, right? It is, if your end goal is self-love. But it isn't if your end goal is to keep people buying more self-help books and wellness products. Interesting, huh?

Most of the books we've lived by also don't have much to say about sexual harassment and abuse. The ones that do tend to tell victims that it's their fault for holding on to hurt and not magically willing themselves to be positive. And a lot of them don't necessarily encourage readers to embrace the bodies they have. Typical books all have pointers, tips, and guidelines on how to be "accountable" to your body by trying to get it "healthy" (a.k.a. skinny), or they blame you for not loving a figure that society tells you is undesirable every day. What these books aren't addressing are the skewed and sexist criteria our current culture has deemed "hot."

These books perpetuate damaging stereotypes, unreachable goals, and self-blame for problems that go way beyond the individual. Because of this we keep feeling like failures, and keep buying more products to fix our unlovable bodies (or at least I do).

I hope that someday soon we'll all laugh about how small-minded we were to give different worth to arbitrary physical traits. But until then we have to find our own ways into loving our bodies. Because, I don't know about you, but I find constantly battling my body and hating myself too tiring to keep up for the rest of my life. Luckily, throughout the run of By the Book, Kristen and I have started to notice a promising trend.

More and more self-help books written by women about self-acceptance and body positivity are popping up. Books like *The Body Is Not an Apology* by Sonya Renee Taylor help shed light on the surreptitious social mores that perpetuate self-doubt and consumerism quick fixes. Reading material like this helps me remember that I'm 100 percent normal for feeling inadequate and that there are structures of ideals in place to make me feel that way. I didn't ask for this; it sought me out.

For me, finding ways to take back control helps. Living by Anuschka Rees's *The Curated Closet* gave me a greater sense of self through exploring how to express my personality as accurately as possible through my garments. *The Body Is Not an Apology* reminded me I can take back control by doing simple things like unsubscribing from social media accounts that make me feel like a trash heap.

I've even gone so far as to get plastic surgery to feel like myself in my body and not like a walking pair of very large breasts. A year after the yellow halter-top debacle, I wasn't doing so hot. From that day on I'd started wearing two bras and layer upon layer of shirts and skipping school almost every day.

When my parents demanded to know what it would take to get me back to school, I didn't have the words to say, "I'm being objectified by a bunch of sexist old dudes in charge of my education and it makes me profoundly uncomfortable." Instead I begged for a breast reduction. And early one summer morning a few months after I turned sixteen, I had the surgery.

I don't remember much because I was heavily drugged— but I do remember waking up and looking down at my bandaged torso and being elated. They were perfect. It felt as though a weight had literally been lifted off my chest.

When I tell people this, a common reaction is to think my parents were fully insane to let their sixteen-year-old get plastic surgery. But I don't care, because after the surgery I felt like my body became mine again. The breasts that had hijacked my life were finally under control, and I was able to finally start making friends with my new adult woman body.

Now plastic surgery is extreme and not for everyone. But

it helped me feel like I belonged in my own body, and to me that's worth it. Because of my surgery, my grades improved, my depression eased up a bit, and I even made the tennis team my senior year. I learned to take pleasure in using my body and exploring it and thinking of it as just as much a part of me as my brain or my personality.

I'm still not the best at being friends with my body. I have to push myself to remember I even like moving it. But I've found that the more I embrace my body and find ways to celebrate it, the more I thrive overall. Seriously, on days I go to yoga or have a good orgasm I'm happier and do way better work. And here's what's fun: making friends with your body can be whatever you want it to be.

Personally, I've found that moving my body with a goal in mind helps me to remember that I'm more than just my thoughts; I'm a human with a badass body that helps my smart-ass mind make its impact on the world. And when I do little things like trying to pamper my skin with a face mask or challenging my balance by attempting to learn how to do headstands in yoga, I'm able to more easily think of my mind and body as two parts of a sickeningly cool whole. Because these little tasks center me and give me enjoyment, I'm more easily able to enjoy my whole self and even love myself.

Keep in mind that everyone is different. My little moments of bodily connection may be totally unappealing to you, and that's a-okay. Kristen loves to connect with herself and her body when she walks in various places around the city or when she's having a picnic outside in the sun with good food and good friends. Her husband, Dean, makes friends with his body by running races and pampering Kristen with foot rubs every morning. Brad, my partner, loves doing big, exciting things like rock climbing or biking the circumference of Manhattan in order to quiet his talkative mind and let his body run the show for a bit.

What I love about learning to make friends with your body is all the extra time and energy you end up with. Turns out self-loathing is a lot of work, and when you're not busy hating yourself you get to focus on tearing apart systems that send you the message to hate yourself. I think Sonya Renee Taylor put it best in *The Body Is Not an Apology*: "Racism, sexism, ableism, homo- and transphobia, ageism, and fatphobia are algorithms created by humans' struggle to make peace with the body. A radical self-love world is a world free from the systems of oppression that make it difficult and sometimes deadly to live in our bodies."

So let's pretend we still think manatees can be mistaken for mermaids, find some ways to make friends with our whole selves, and save up all those negative thoughts for things that actually suck instead of our bodies.

Dear Kristen and Jolenta,

It's really easy for Jolenta, a tall, slim, able-bodied white woman, to say "make peace with your body." A lot of us have bodies that the world treats like the enemy—black bodies, fat bodies, bodies that are in wheelchairs. A lot of us have the world telling us on a daily basis to hate ourselves. What do you have to say to people like me?

—JL

Dear JL,

You are right, it is a lot easier for me to run my mouth about how amazing it is to embrace a body that doesn't stray too far from our society's annoying made-up standard of "normal." And you are super-right that the world is brutal and constantly reminding us all that we are unworthy of love because our bodies will never be enough. And this message is compounded and magnified in ways I can never even fathom to people who happen to have been born in bodies that don't look or function like my own.

All I can say is that I'm a "burn it down" kind of woman. If the world is against something, I consider working hard to love that something instead of hating it to be an act of rebellion. Badass rebels who are brave enough to love their bodies in the face of the hate given off by the world could inspire others around them to start rebelling themselves, and then maybe someday in the near future we'll have a wild self-love revolution on our hands. Maybe I'm getting carried away now, but I think you catch my drift.

—Jolenta

DON'T LET YOUR VIRGINITY STORY DEFINE YOU

Kristen

You know how romance novels and rom-coms and sitcoms and religion and pretty much all of society tell girls that losing our virginity should be something special? On the more benign end of the spectrum, the message is "Give your virginity only to someone you love, someone you'll think of fondly when you reminisce about your first time." On the more extreme end, the message is "No man wants a chewed-up piece of gum. Your vagina is the gum, and your future husband deserves an unchewed piece."

And so, a lot of us walk through our youth holding our virginity in very high regard—so high that it borders on idolatry. We absorb and sometimes even agree with misogynistic messages about girls who aren't "selective enough" about who they have sex with. And we hold high hopes and serious expectations that our own first times will be beautiful, transcendent, even sacred.

I certainly felt this way when I was young. I desperately longed for love. I wanted a boyfriend. I wanted to have sex with this imaginary boyfriend with whom I was so much in love. Our first time would, of course, be perfect. We would both have lots of orgasms. Afterward, we would hold each other close. Down the road, we might get married. Or maybe we wouldn't. Regardless, I'd be happy that I didn't blow my one chance to do things right with a rando who didn't love me.

But this isn't how things went. The first time I had sex was in a car. And it was with my boss. I was a junior in high school, and up until that point, not a single boy had ever flirted with me, complimented me on my appearance, or asked me out. On the rare occasions boys approached me smiling, it was to ask if I'd introduce them to one of my prettier friends.

Then I began working at a restaurant in my neighborhood. I loved the food at the restaurant and I loved my job as a cashier and hostess. Most of all, I adored my coworkers. Most of us were in our teens and twenties. A few were in their thirties. We all got along brilliantly. And one staffer in particular loved to flirt with the rest of us. He was the headwaiter, the one who put together the weekly schedules, and the one I talked to if I needed a day off or an extra shift. Before him, I didn't know what it felt like to have a man call me pretty. And I ate it up, even though I knew it was wildly inappropriate for a man I reported to—a man who was ten years older and also flirted with everyone else—to talk to me the way he did.

One night, a few months after I'd started my job at the restaurant, this boss offered to give me a ride home. Mind you, I lived only a fifteen-minute walk away. But I agreed, and in my heart, I knew there was a good chance we'd make out. Prior to this, I'd had almost zero experience with any boy. I was excited.

And so, when he pulled the car over on a dirt road, and he leaned across to kiss me, I was thrilled. And then there was touching. And then, before I even really realized what was happening, we were having sex. There was no talk of a condom. It wasn't romantic. It hurt. And it lasted less than the length of a single pop song that I still hate to this day. I was utterly confused. How had I let this happen? Wasn't this exactly how I didn't want to lose my virginity?

Afterward, I tried my best to rationalize my confusion away. When my boss asked to meet up with me on two more occasions, I agreed, telling myself these horrible hookup sessions were real dates. When I told the story about losing my virginity back to myself, I'd point to these "dates" and think, *We were clearly in a relationship.*

And then, at the beginning of my senior year of high school, my family moved away. Before we did, I gave my boss my Nanna's phone number and address. I prayed that he would call me and write me letters, that maybe we could have a long-distance romance. Of course, I never heard from him again.

For years afterward, when people asked about how I lost my virginity, I'd downplay how horrible it was. I was embarrassed. Embarrassed for giving away something so special to someone who was clearly so undeserving. Embarrassed for being so desperate to rewrite my story that I went back for more.

But here's the thing I know now, decades later: It doesn't really matter how I lost my virginity. Now, I'm not saying this as a way to let my old boss off the hook. I absolutely think he violated codes of basic human decency and broke a lot of labor laws by doing what he did to me and with me. I hope—for the sake of all women and girls—that after me, he cut off his own testicles.

What I mean is, this one act of sex didn't define me. It didn't ruin me. It didn't set the stage for all future sexual relationships. It didn't make me distasteful to future partners. It didn't imprint me with only one memory to look back on forever. I am no more or less lovable because of that three minutes in that boss's sedan on that dirt road—or because of any other act of sex I've had in my life.

I wish I'd realized this back then. But at that point, my frame of reference was small. That single event seemed huge. And the world at large was still sending the message that the most monumental mistake I could make in my young life was to lose my virginity the wrong way.

And sadly, a lot of that messaging still exists. Bestselling self-help books like Rachel Hollis's *Girl, Wash Your Face* make it clear that there's a right way and a wrong way for a girl to lose her virginity. Hollis, in particular, says that "good Christian girls" engage in sex only after exchanging wedding vows with their husbands—and frames the fact that she had sex with her husband before marriage as a story of guilt. But if she, a woman who married the first and only man she ever slept with, has grappled with guilt over how she lost her virginity, where does that leave the rest of us, who lost our virginity to people who were predatory, or maybe just not "the one"? The answer: with a cross to bear and a lifetime of shame.

But it doesn't have to be this way. Sex isn't something that runs out. It's not like a chewed-up piece of gum. There's almost always more that can be had, and other people with whom it can be had. And having sex with someone horrible or forgettable the first time doesn't mean *you* are horrible or forgettable.

And speaking of horrible, can we be frank? First-time sex is usually pretty bad, no matter who it's with. It's often awkward, and there are usually not a lot of orgasms to go around. That's because it takes a while to learn a partner's body and to learn what feels good to you with each person you get it on with. This is true whether it's your first partner ever or your first partner this week.

Only one self-help book Jolenta and I have read has bothered to mention this: *Next Level Basic: The Definitive Basic Bitch Handbook,* by Stassi Schroeder. Now mind you, this is not a great book. [Jolenta: Speak for yourself, Kristen! I love this book!] It presumes that the reader is white and blond and rich and has the same problems as the white, blond, rich author. [Jolenta: Okay, yes, there is that.] But the book does get a couple things right, and one of those things is that first-time sex is overrated. Schroeder talks frankly about her first time: from not knowing what to do with her body to not knowing what to say to the guy before, during, and after. And she does her best to demystify the whole affair.

Why don't more books do this? Why don't more books send girls (and boys!) the message that while sex can certainly be transcendent, it's sometimes not, especially the first time?

And why don't we allow ourselves the same grace with first-time sex that we give ourselves when we do other things for the first time, like take our first steps, or write our names, or cook our first meals? We teeter and fall over within seconds of taking our first steps. Our first attempts at writing are scribbles. Our first meals are unexceptional. And that's fine. That's normal. Those first few minutes and seconds of trying something new don't ruin us. And sex is no different.

Yes, my first time having sex was lousy. But it didn't ruin me. It certainly didn't define me. And Jolenta assures me that losing her virginity didn't ruin her either.

P.S. I think it's important to note that the entire definition of virginity is highly contested—at least culturally speaking. For example, are people no longer virgins if their hymens were broken during a nonsexual activity, or if they were born with partial hymens? Are people still virgins if the sex they partake of is nonpenetrative, or if the penetration is anal, rather than vaginal? Are people who've been raped, but never had consensual sex, still virgins? Where do people who engage in same-sex activities fall on the virginity scale, if virginity is only about penises and vaginas? All our blurry definitions of virginity are just one more reason I believe we should be fixating on virginity less—and consent, pleasure, and autonomy more.

Dear Kristen and Jolenta,

What if the way I lost my virginity was traumatizing? Are you telling me to just be okay with that?
—CG

Dear CG,

No, not at all! You never, ever have to be okay with that. I consider my first "attempted" time to be traumatic and I still work through issues associated with it sixteen years later. I will never be okay with it. Sexual assault and traumatizing experiences are never okay.

Personally, I'm working on not letting trauma define me or my sexuality, and that's what we're trying to get at here. The traumatic things that happen to us are horrible and undeserved, but sometimes, if you're like me at least, you might get stuck thinking you did deserve it, and then it starts to define everything you do and who you think you are as a person. And for me, being okay with not defining myself by my sexual trauma was superfreeing.

We're sorry losing your virginity was traumatic; no one deserves that. And we would never tell you how to feel about it, but we definitely don't want you to beat yourself up over it. And we're sorry if that's what we made you think!
—Jolenta

HAVE THINGS
TO LOOK
FORWARD TO

Kristen

When I was twenty-nine years old, I was for the most part incredibly happy. I had fantastic friends, a nice apartment, and the best boyfriend I'd had up until that point. I felt good about how I looked and good about the life I'd created for myself. I loved my city and I loved my life.

But as I approached my thirtieth birthday, I wanted to be prepared for the worst. I had friends who, on their thirtieth birthdays, were overcome with an enormous sense of sadness; friends who said they realized they weren't where they thought they'd be at that point in their lives; friends who felt they'd thrown away their youth. What if I woke up on the morning of my thirtieth birthday and felt the same way? What if I freaked out?

And so I created a thirtieth birthday first-aid kit. The kit consisted of one thing: a list. The list was long, and made up entirely of things I considered accomplishments—from paying my way through college to starting grad school to saving up a proper emergency fund. It included all the places I'd lived, all the places I'd traveled to, and all the jobs I'd held. And it also included less tangible things, like the joy I felt over my wide and deep circle of friends, my close relationships with the women in my family, and the work I'd done for my own mental and physical health over the years.

After compiling my list, I proudly told my friend Linda about it. And when I did, I expected her to pat me on the back and offer to buy me a drink. But rather than applaud my efforts, she looked at me quizzically. "Kristen," she said, "I don't know about this list."

"You don't know?" What was there not to know? How could she not see that my list was an act of ingenuity? I may as well have told her that I put on socks all by myself that day.

But then she followed up her ho-hum words with advice that I'll never forget: "Your list is fine and good. But instead of looking backward, what would happen if you looked forward? What are some of the amazing things you'll do after you turn thirty? I imagine that list will be a lot longer than the list you already made."

My first thought was *Oh my god, Linda, you are brilliant.* My second thought was *This is going to be so much fun!* And wasn't fun what I really needed for my thirtieth birthday first-aid kit, even more than a sense of pride?

I got to work listing places I would visit, financial milestones I would reach, foods I would eat, and books I would read (notably, none of them had anything to do with self-help). I dreamed big, picturing myself walking around the markets of Thailand. And I also dreamed of things I couldn't quite picture: like working a job I was passionate about.

But making my list wasn't just about dreaming, it was about so many other things. Being a lover of research, I used my list making as an excuse to learn more about everything that piqued my interest—from classic movies to historic sites to bird-watching and gardening. All the learning made my brain tingle with happiness.

My "looking-forward" list also reminded me of the importance of novelty. When we're living our day-in, day-out lives, it's easy to fall into a rut. That rut can feel comfortable. But it can also keep us from growing, being challenged, and experiencing a genuine sense of surprise in the world. Surprises are great! And in writing out my list, I realized nearly all of it was made up of new experiences, which came with the potential for many surprises.

What's more, my list making instilled in me a sense of anticipation, one of my very favorite emotional states. Like most kids, I counted down the days to school ending each summer and school beginning again each fall. Back in my single days, I adored the days and weeks of not having sex with a new paramour, while looking forward to it. And each year, I try to maximize my holiday anticipation, by beginning my countdown to Christmas the day after Halloween.

Perhaps most important, Linda's looking-forward list idea was centered on hope and optimism. By writing a list for the future, we say, "Yes, there will be a future." We say, "There are good things ahead." We proclaim, "There's a lot to live for, and I'm excited about those things."

Now, Linda, of course, did not invent the idea of looking-forward lists. In fact, a few of the books we've lived by have had their own versions of these lists. But truth be told, their versions are both (a) wildly amorphous and (b) hard to put into practice.

On the amorphous front: Books like *The Secret,* by Rhonda Byrne, encourage us to create vision boards of what we dream of—from luxury items to fantasy vacations—but they don't give us a concrete list that can be added to or subtracted from. And on top of that, they're tied to the aforementioned Law of Attraction—meaning these vision boards are more reliant on the universe giving us what we dream of than on us making the dreams come true ourselves. Where's the sense of fun and challenge in that?

In terms of lists that are hard to put into practice, *The 4-Hour Workweek,* by Tim Ferriss, provides a very clear example. Ferriss's list includes mastering competitive horseback archery, starring in films in Asia, becoming a world-class martial artist, and living in some of the world's most remote places (to name just a few items). On top of that, Ferriss believes we shouldn't wait until retirement to do all the things we dream of. We should spread those dreams throughout our lives. But most of us can't do this. Most of us work a lot, have very little vacation time, and are dealing with limited financial resources. Very few people can take months off their jobs to become master horseback archers.

The beauty of my friend Linda's advice is that it's simple, clear, practical, and personal. And that means just about anyone can do it—including people with Ferriss's resources or people with mine. It can be enlisted by people who are turning thirty, and also by people turning fourteen or eighty-two. Regardless of whether we are in a good place or a bad place in our lives, in miserable jobs or satisfying ones, most of us can dream, and most of us can make lists.

Of course, making lists of things to look forward to can also be a team sport. The act of dreaming about, then planning, then anticipating a girls' trip or a romantic weekend away can provide hours of mutual joy between friends and partners. It can give people who love each other a shared vocabulary of dreams. And it can remind people that they're united in joy, not just toil. Jolenta and I wouldn't have started our podcasts or written this book together had we not first brainstormed and written down what we were looking forward to.

One last thing: As I see it, it doesn't even matter if we do most of the things on our looking-forward lists. It's fine if we do just a few. More important is that we're engaging with our fantasies and keeping an eye out for new things to dream about, and above all, reminding ourselves that there is a lot to be excited about in the future, regardless of what we've done or not done in the past.

ACCEPT THAT MEDS ARE FINE

Jolenta

Do you ever have that dream where you're trying to dial a phone and no matter how hard you focus you cannot make your fingers press the right numbers and you keep having to dial over and over again? Even if you don't have that dream, I think you get how frustrating a dream like that would feel. That feeling, that fuzziness of the mind, that inability to function correctly no matter how hard you try, is something I've carried with me for as long as I can remember.

The first time this fuzziness got me in trouble I was in kindergarten. It was early on in the school year and I had been playing with a classmate in the sandbox. We were really hitting it off, mapping out make-believe horse trails in the sand with our fingers and talking about the horses we wished we had. The world around us vanished as we played, but our little fun bubble was burst by a parent helper. She ran up to us huffing and puffing, her face was all red, and she yelled, "Where were you girls?" Oops! We had accidentally lost track of time, not heard the bell, missed a lesson, and now it was time to go home!

Incidents like this just kept happening to me. In third grade I wasn't allowed to keep water bottles or markers in my desk because, instead of doing my schoolwork, I had a habit of accidentally focusing on making tie-dyed tissue papers through an intricate system of washable marker dots and water drops. During my freshman year of high school I had so much trouble focusing on the board through my mind fog, I ended up getting glasses to see if that would help. In college I was either a party girl or the hardest working in my class, there was no in-between. I was pulling all-nighters to write detailed papers or out dancing and trying various drugs until the wee hours of the morning. When I got my first job, I would cry every morning as I got ready because my fuzz-addled mind found office work so monotonous I was miserable. And because I seemed to be the only one feeling like my soul was being sucked out, I felt like a failure, too. Everyone else seemed to get by just fine.

Nearly two years ago, Brad was talking about feeling like this at work to our couples therapist. This would be a good time to point out that Brad and I are very similar when it comes to how frustratingly unable to focus our minds we can be. After listening to Brad for a while our therapist turned to him and said what he was describing sounded a lot like attention-deficit/hyperactivity disorder.

When she said this I laughed to myself and thought, *Oh man, if Brad might have ADHD, there's a strong chance I'm in the same boat. My mind is way more all over the place than his. He's the one that's focused and has it together!*

With my curiosity piqued, I made an appointment with

a psychiatrist who accepted my insurance. She talked to me for over an hour about my life, my struggles, what Brad and I had just discussed in therapy. And she also had me take some tests. When our time was up she confirmed my suspicions and said that fuzzy, hard-to-control brain of mine was an ADHD brain.

When I started taking medication for ADHD at thirty-one, the effects blew me away. My thoughts were so clear and easy to control. I felt superhuman, as if I were taking magic "easy way out" pills.

A few months into the process of figuring out which drug and dosage worked best for me, I let my psychiatrist in on my secret during a visit to her office. "My mind is so unobstructed and my thoughts are so linear. Is this okay? I think I'm cheating," I said with embarrassment.

I gazed out the window at the midtown Manhattan skyline, afraid to look my psychiatrist in the eye. And I waited for her to say I must be on the wrong meds, because no one is allowed to feel as clearheaded as I did right then.

But instead she said this: "You're not cheating. You're just finally reaching the level playing field."

Interesting. This was not the response I was expecting. I turned to look at her as she continued talking. She was smiling, but there was a serious tone in her voice.

"Would you say someone who took heart medication to make their heart function better is cheating?" she asked.

"No, of course not," I answered.

"Right," she said. "And would you call an asthmatic

who takes a puff of an inhaler when they're having trouble breathing a cheater?"

"No, that would be dumb."

"Then I guess you can't call someone who takes daily medication because neurotransmitters don't function properly a cheater, can you? And that's all you are."

Oh snap! She was right! I wasn't a cheater. I was simply someone whose brain either doesn't produce enough dopamine or has too few dopamine receptors. I take medication to remedy this deficiency and function more neurotypically.

That conversation totally changed how I saw my situation. I wasn't cheating. I was simply taking care of my body, helping it to function the way it is supposed to. I'll pass on the idea that taking medication makes you weak. And a hard pass on the idea that taking care of the body part known as the brain is somehow more taboo than caring for the heart or the liver or a penis with erectile dysfunction.

Most of the self-help books Kristen and I have come across don't mention medications like SSRIs and stimulants. And the ones we've read that do mention drugs do it in the context of becoming so "well" that they're no longer needed. Surprisingly, *The Nature Fix,* by Florence Williams, was one of these books. While reading a chapter about boys at an outdoor academy being "cured" of their ADHD, I was stunned that a book about the benefits of wandering through forests and smelling the ocean air was taking the time to pooh-pooh medication. I couldn't help but take it personally when I read the story of the boy profiled in the chapter. Williams describes the process of finding medication that's a good fit as a harrowing montage of poison pills being fed to a child. Now, I'm not saying this is never the case. Nor am I saying it's cool to simply throw meds toward any behavioral issue before investigating what deeper issues are causing someone to act out. But speaking as someone of the female persuasion, someone whose gender wasn't studied until recently in regard to ADHD and brain chemistry, I feel lucky to have been diagnosed. And after thirty-two years of wondering what was wrong with me, I feel beyond lucky to be able to afford and take medication that helps my slow neurotransmitters get up to speed.

Reading that chapter in *The Nature Fix* about people curing something that took me more than thirty years to even figure out was an issue wasn't fun. While it's a common notion that ADHD is overdiagnosed and meds are over-prescribed, this belief is based on data that have predominantly come from studies of little white boys. Historically the disorder has been considered a "male" affliction. When one hears those four initials, ADHD, one often thinks of a little guy bouncing off the walls, making life hard for everyone around him in his second-grade class. But once the medical community started studying women and girls, they came to realize that their diagnostic criteria didn't catch ADHD in most women and young girls.

Once researchers and physicians began studying ADHD in women, they found the disorder presented in profoundly different ways. Since young girls are often socialized to not burden others with their problems and instead be quiet, supportive caregivers, they aren't always running around or talking nonstop. They're labeled as spacey daydreamers, constantly scolded for having their heads in the clouds and not living up to their potential.

On top of that, the testosterone that floods boys' bodies when they hit puberty often lessens their symptoms of ADHD. So it's considered a children's condition that one should be able to "grow out of." But here's the fun part: Estrogen, that cute chemical that floods female bodies during puberty, exacerbates the symptoms of ADHD. So when young women with undiagnosed ADHD reach their tween years and suddenly begin having a harder and harder time in school, they're already considered "too old" to even have the disorder. Currently a child has to exhibit symptoms before the age of twelve to be diagnosed. My symptoms began disrupting my life and education around the age of fourteen.

Instead of being helped, nurtured, diagnosed, or medicated like their louder and more disruptive male classmates, these young women go undiagnosed their entire childhoods and are often simply labeled underachievers for the rest of their lives. And this doesn't even begin to cover those of us who don't fall on one end or the other of the gender identity scale. The medical community doesn't seem to have touched those identifying as intersex, nonbinary, genderqueer, trans, and so on. I don't feel comfortable with the idea of discounting the benefits of medication when there are large groups of people not being studied or prioritized by the medical community. Until every person and body can be treated with equality, understanding, and compassion, how can a self-help author feel confident enough to make such bold proclamations about how using medications like antidepressants and stimulants affects the brain?

When science catches up, and starts looking at brains of people other than Caucasian men, I'll be much more willing to read generalized advice on the subject. But until then I'd rather my psychiatrist, a person who knows me and my medical history well, give me advice on when (if ever) I stop taking medication.

The medical community now refers to women like myself, who don't get diagnosed until well into adulthood, as the "lost generation" of ADHD. Our potential was squashed, our neurological wiring considered a chosen shortcoming instead of something far beyond our control. We're lost because the medical and educational structures around us found it easier to assume we were stupid or simply lacking instead of looking into why we were underperforming. But somehow those same institutions saw all the value in the world in little boy brains. And if those boys were struggling in school, there was obviously something medically wrong behind *their* lack of productivity. Because they're all superior, high-functioning geniuses by default, right? Ew, no thank you.

My diagnosis took me from being lost to being found. I was just beginning to explore how amazing it felt to be able to choose what I worked on when I started my workday instead of struggling to begin and stay on task every few minutes. I had no idea that people just walked around choosing what they put their attention on! And I didn't enjoy a book saying my problems might be solved if I'd sat in a tree longer. In fact, taking ADHD medication helped me to appreciate the nature around me way more than I used to. When I walked down the street on my new meds, I noticed everything around me in more detail. The leaves on the trees were greener, flowers were more vibrant, bumblebees were even cuter and fuzzier. So it was a huge bummer that a book about the benefits of being in nature, which I believe in strongly, was taking a stand against ADHD medicine. And citing a story about little white boys as the reason for this stance? I mean, come on! I didn't know irony could feel this personally insulting.

I figure any book that shames you for something out of your control, like brain chemistry, is probably not "helping" much. So it's not really self-help, as far as I'm concerned. I'll take my advice from books that give constructive advice and don't make general claims about such individualized things as one's medication.

So instead of fretting over whether or not I'll stop taking medication for my ADHD, or my anxiety for that matter, I'm going to live my life and pat myself on the back for being a good, responsible body inhabitant who cares for every part of herself, brain and all. I highly suggest you do the same; it's way more fun and productive than calling yourself a cheater for taking care of yourself.

SEE A THERAPIST

Jolenta

Some of the most amazing people in my life are people I pay to talk to me. That's right, I'm talking about therapists, psychiatrists, and other mental-health-care professionals!

While this sounds funny, I assure you it's not a joke. All the self-help books in the world could never do what therapy has done for me in terms of personal growth and understanding how my past influences my present. No matter how good the advice in books I've come across is, it would be useless to me without a trained professional to help me contextualize it and put it into action.

I'll be real with you—I'm going through a hell of a time right now. If it weren't for therapy I wouldn't be out of bed today, let alone writing this book right now. A little over a year ago my family fell apart. My parents split because my dad had been secretly giving millions of dollars to a failing startup he had invested in. The money he gave them was essentially stolen from my mother. He gave half of their hard-earned life savings away to strangers behind her back.

A few months after they split up I stopped hearing from

my dad. This was disappointing, because he himself said he wanted to have weekly Sunday calls with me. But as every Sunday came around, he was silent. I suspected it was because he was dating someone and he didn't want to tell me about it.

Now, the thing is, I know adults date, and I think it's fine for him to dip his toes back into the dating pool. I even told him that he should do whatever he wanted as long as he was transparent with me. And I needed that transparency. After all his duplicity, I didn't have much trust in him. So whenever I would get ahold of him, I'd ask over and over if he was dating. But instead he just locked me out and kept more secrets.

Turns out, weeks after my mom got her own place, he started seriously dating a woman with a teenage daughter. By the time I found out, he'd been with this woman for half a year. If my mom hadn't figured this out by accident I'd still be in the dark about the fact that while he barely called me he was spending his time and the little money he had left on a secret replacement woman and daughter—going on trips, cooking meals, and even spending most of the holidays with them.

This has been heartbreaking. I'm an only child. My three-person family was so close that my friends used to joke that we had never even heard of boundaries. So on top of my little triangle of love collapsing, I completely lost my father to his new replacement family a few months later. I feel incredibly abandoned.

This betrayal feels so massive that currently I'm not

speaking to him, and I'm considering cutting him out of my life completely. Why am I telling you all of this? Partially because I'm still fuming with rage and it's all I can think about. But mostly to illustrate how specific life's garbage usually is. My problems are run-of-the-mill; plenty of dads are distant with some undiagnosed issues that make them selfish monsters. And actually, I'm quite lucky to be able to even complain about my daddy issues and how they hurt my feelings. But still, there is no self-help guide for this exact problem. Sadly, I can't pop out to my local independently owned bookstore to pick up a copy of *Girl, Sorry Your Dad Picked Bad Investments and Secretly Replaced You and Your Mom!*

But I can go to a therapist to work through some of my rage and pain and old hurt feelings. Therapists are truly the best. They are literal experts in family drama and the self-loathing that often comes with it. No self-help book can replace a conversation with a human who went to school to help you gain the skills you need to successfully navigate through life. My ability to even acknowledge the fiery rage mentioned in the previous paragraph is because of a wonderful woman with an office in the West Village. A woman who (mercifully) takes my insurance and meager copay to let me sit on her couch and very slowly work through that same messy stuff we get hit with by life from time to time.

Most of the self-help books Kristen and I have lived by mention going to therapy as a footnote. It's mentioned at the ends of chapters tucked back in the last few pages of the books that touch on the topic and it's often referred to as an extreme measure to take if you're so messed up, the book isn't enough to help you cope. This sentiment is garbage. Seeking help is not a cop-out; it's being smart. Why consider talking to an actual expert in life-coping skills a last resort?

I'm not sure what's going to happen with my dad. But I sleep easier every night knowing that I have a supersmart woman who specializes in my kind of messy in my corner helping me figure this all out.

Dear Kristen and Jolenta,

I was brought up to see therapy in one of two ways: (1) as something only the most messed up people did—people who were institutionalized and not in their right minds or (2) as something neurotic, narcissistic people did—people without real problems who would rather live in their heads than go out and take control of their lives. Logically speaking, I know this is wrong. And I think I could definitely benefit from some therapy myself. But I can't seem to get my logical brain to override all that messaging I received growing up.

—NT

Dear NT,

Full disclosure: That messaging you received growing up wasn't totally wrong. Yes, some truly messed up people go to therapy. And yes, some neurotic, narcissistic people go to therapy. But on top of that, people who lose jobs go to therapy. People who are going through breakups go to therapy. So do people who have a hard time sleeping and people who feel they tend to self-sabotage and people who have a hard time living in the moment and people who just want to make sense of the weird messages they received growing up.

On the flip side, some truly messed up people never go to therapy. And some neurotic, narcissistic people never go to therapy either. Therapy is not an all-or-nothing game in which all the people we were taught to look down on go to lie on a couch, while the rest of us live in the real world.

But I trust that you already know this, NT. You've already said that, logically speaking, you know the messages you received about therapy growing up were wrong.

And so, I'm going to suggest you look at things differently. Rather than see therapists as their own weird unique thing outside your purview, maybe try seeing them as one more kind of specialist on your team of healthcare experts. I'm guessing you have a dentist for your oral health, and maybe a dermatologist for your skin health, and some other doctors who help you manage your well-being.

Some of these specialists you see regularly, for ongoing issues. Some you see only in emergencies. Some you see annually or semiannually for maintenance. A therapist is no different. You may see one for a few weeks or months. You may see one only during moments of crisis. But regardless, afterward, you hopefully feel better.

One last thing: Therapy isn't for everyone. And the fact that Jolenta and I have benefited from it doesn't mean we think everyone else has to go to therapy, too. But if the only thing holding you back from it is a fear that it's beneath you, we assure you: It's no more beneath you to see a therapist than it is to see an allergist. It may even be the best thing you do for your health.

—Kristen

CONCLUSION

Jolenta and Kristen

JOLENTA: Now that we've lived by fifty self-help books, people often want to know: What's the big takeaway? Have you learned the meaning of life or the secret to happiness? What have all these books taught you?

KRISTEN: Long story short: not much.

JOLENTA: I'm pretty sure that's not true.

KRISTEN: I'm not saying I'm incapable of learning. But I can say this: Before embarking on this adventure with you, I already knew not to give all my trust to self-anointed gurus. I knew there wasn't a single meaning of life, but rather a million meanings. I knew there wasn't one right answer for how to be productive or how to experience love or how to connect with other humans or be how to be creative or how to feel at peace.

JOLENTA: No one is more of an expert in you than you.

KRISTEN: Yes! Why would people who've never met you, who've never talked at length with you about your issues, who are clueless about your backstory and medical history and life—why would those somebodies know better than you about how to be you?

JOLENTA: Obviously, they wouldn't. But I totally understand the instinct to trust these writers. You and I both know I've been drawn to them plenty over the course of my life.

KRISTEN: Hold on. This actually gets to something important I've learned during the course of our experiment: I think I've learned to be more empathetic.

JOLENTA: You've always been empathetic.

KRISTEN: Yes and no. I have loads of empathy for you, for my loved ones, and for people in the most general sense, but before By the Book, I didn't have a lot of empathy for people who devoured self-help books. Honestly, I saw them as gullible fools. I wondered how they could fall so easily for fad diets, fake promises, and snake-oil salesman taglines like "the only guaranteed way to change your life." But you helped change my mind about that. And so did our listeners.

JOLENTA: We have the best listeners. Listeners, if you're reading this: Know that we love you. We love that you write us by the hundreds each week to tell us about your lives, your insecurities, the problems you've faced, and why you sometimes turn to self-help books to get answers. Plus, we love all the photos you send us of your nature fixes and dogs in clothes.

KRISTEN: Yes, thank you. In addition to helping me put human faces and names to all the self-help readers out there, you've helped me to understand why people seek out these books in the first place. I mean, intellectually speaking, I knew why: Our mainstream medical systems don't dedicate a lot of resources to the understanding of mental health; our social structures and economic systems don't lend themselves to people caring for and getting to know themselves; most people don't even get paid time off to have a kid or mourn the loss of a loved one, much less see a psychiatrist or get enough sleep. It's understandable why people needing help would just grab a book.

But beyond the intellectual level, this is what I've come to terms with: Sometimes when we're lost, any kind of direction can feel like a way toward something, even if the person giving us directions is just holding up a picture of an arrow that points at the ground.

JOLENTA: Right, and on top of that, I think most people feel lost some of the time. Or if you're like me, you feel lost most of the time. In our current culture, and in America, in particular, there's not a lot of space for people who don't feel okay. Confidence and extroversion and having it all—these are qualities we often mistake as synonymous with success. We often gloss over the fact that even the most confident people don't start out that way or feel confident all the time. And on top of that we often consider acknowledging anything negative or asking for help to be weakness—when really it's usually the first step toward positive change. You can't change things you never choose to acknowledge. And hey, if I hadn't been open about how unhappy I was, I would have never even thought of making By the Book with my amazing friend, Kristen!

KRISTEN: Aw, that's so sweet. I wish the world told us more often, "It's okay to not be okay. It's normal. And it's great to get help." Long story short, I no longer see all self-help enthusiasts as suckers.

JOLENTA: Weirdly, I've become more fascinated by self-help authors themselves during this process. And to be honest, I've kind of come around to your way of thinking about some of these people shilling advice.

KRISTEN: How so?

JOLENTA: Real talk, a lot of them are complete frauds. I'm not just talking about the ones with degrees from diploma mills. Some of these authors are less self-help leaders than marketing geniuses who tap into whatever cultural moment is at hand. One minute the author is a pickup artist, the next he's writing books on how to self-actualize. And even with the most well-intentioned ones, there's a tendency to overstate promises, or to offer advice that's just one obsessive person's quirky way of self-soothing.

KRISTEN: So many authors seem to fall into that last category. They found something to fixate on that prevents them from going off the deep end—a method of obsessive cleaning, a repetitive set of tasks to complete before the sun comes up, meditating for two hours a day. But who are they to say that their personal pacifier is a fix-all? What makes them think it would apply to a general audience?

JOLENTA: And speaking of general audiences, let's talk facts: Two thirds of self-help readers are women. Two thirds of authors are men. At least, that's what a study of Goodreads self-help books found. And our own research indicates that most self-help authors are white. A very large percentage are well-to-do. And way too many have tunnel vision. They don't know what it's like to be a woman or poor or a person of color. And yet they're saying things like "If I could do it, so can you."

KRISTEN: Yeah, it's really easy for you to say that, dude, when you were born on third base. I don't even own a pair of baseball cleats.

JOLENTA: Exactly. And that's assuming you even want to be like these self-proclaimed experts—many of whom preach superficial values and worship consumer-minded symbols of success.

KRISTEN: All things that don't actually help people like me—or a lot of people, for that matter—enjoy life more or find happiness.

JOLENTA: Yeah. I tend to think if a book is telling you that you should want the life the author has, you should be wary of the advice. Those authors are setting themselves up as idols, not helpers.

KRISTEN: I agree. Also, watch out for books that make you feel bad. If what you're reading encourages you to call yourself a failure or blame yourself for bad stuff that comes your way, feel free to put it down.

JOLENTA: One of the most surprising things about living by all of these books is how much advice I've discovered I don't like. Turns out knowing what you hate and trying something new that rubs you the wrong way can teach you a ton about yourself. I know I hate being told to forgive, I hate when men advise me not to take things personally, I hate waking up early simply because doing so connotes drive in our society. These are all new facts I've learned about myself. And the more I know about what I don't like, the closer I get to figuring out what actually works for me and what tips I do want to implement to make my life more enjoyable.

KRISTEN: I love that. Even when advice feels futile, you can still learn something about yourself. It just may not be what the author thought you would learn. I'm learning that it's all about being kind. The advice that really inspires me is about spreading compassion and acting with grace—whether it's how I deal with myself, my loved ones, my community, or even the planet.

JOLENTA: So when it comes down to it, I say do you and be open to finding new parts of you. But don't forget to trust your gut. You are the ultimate authority on yourself and what works for you. Just because it's in a book and works for some people, don't freak out if you aren't enlightened by every self-help book you read. It doesn't mean you're broken; the advice might just be shitty.

KRISTEN: And don't try to seek out perfection. Don't believe anyone who tells you there's a secret way to be happy all the time. Life is way more complex and interesting than a single emotion.

JOLENTA: We know you've got this.

KRISTEN: You're going to be fine.

ACKNOWLEDGMENTS

Jolenta

First, I have to thank Kristen Meinzer. Who knew becoming friends over bickering about movies at work would lead to all of this? You are an inspiration and you keep me grounded. Thank you for always being you and for telling stories with me.

Liz Parker, our agent, you plucked us out of obscurity and helped us achieve things I never even thought to dream of. Thank you for believing in us and fighting the good fight for us along with everyone else at Verve.

Cassie Jones, you are the best editor someone who knows nothing about writing books could ask for. Your gentle guidance and enthusiastic encouragement made this process a delight. And to everyone at William Morrow, thanks for taking a chance on a self-help reality show podcast—it's been a dream come true.

To everyone who's worked on By the Book from its inception to now, thank you from the bottom of my heart. Cameron Drews, Mia Lobel, and Laura Mayer: Because of you we got the most kick-ass start ever. Your input and storytelling chops shaped the show's entire format and vibe. Nora Ritchie, Casey Holford, Chris Bannon, and the rest of the Stitcher team: You all have become our home away from home. Your expertise, craft, and hard work shine through in everything we make together. Lindsey Kratochwill, thank you for holding down the We Love You (And So Can You) fort while we write this. And Dean McRobie, thank you for supporting Kristen and me while letting us record how our projects disrupt your life. You are so giving and such a delight.

Thank you to the mentors I've had: Peter Novak, Ken Sonkin, Arwa Gunja, Ellen Frankman, Jay Cowit, Kevin Allison, and Charles Tuthill. Each of you took the time to see me, believe in me, teach me, and push me to do the best work possible. For this, I'll always be grateful. And special thank-you shout-outs also go to Caroline and Rachelle.

To all of my friends, thank you. Especially those of you who've put up with me while I live by books or just while I was a hot mess: Elspeth Macmillan, Natalie Fish, Sasha Borodovsky, Peter Bean, Alex Harris, Melissa Callahan, Chloe Dixon, Erica Smith, Janna Emig, Chloe Hughes, Ben Lasser, Mattie Ettenheim, Courtney Byrne-Mitchell, Zach and Vicky Topkis, Amit Elhanan, Sophie Marks, Katie McNish, Chris Pappas, and Michelle Onufrak. Thank you for inspiring me, laughing at my jokes, and enduring whatever I'm obsessed with at the moment.

Thanks also to my family. To my aunts, uncles, and grandparents, thank you for believing in me and being there for me, especially recently. Suzanne Greenberg, thank you for being my biggest fan since the second you met me. You are my sunshine. I'm funny only because of you. Brad Mielke, thank you for knowing what I'm capable of even when I don't. Without your love and enthusiasm, I probably wouldn't have even started this project. And little Frank, you're the best dog and home-office mate anyone could ask for.

Mostly I have to thank listeners of By the Book. This book is for you. Thank you for identifying with our stories and sharing your own. The By the Book community has become a magical place full of celebrations and support, and it's a joy to be a part of. I hope this book does you proud.

Kristen

This book never would have happened without the great Jolenta Greenberg. Jolenta, thank you for asking me years ago to host a wacky show about self-help books with you, and for being patient with me when it didn't happen at first, and for being fantastic once it did. Working with you on By the Book, and on everything that's spun off of it, has been a joy and the best kind of learning experience. You and the show have made my life better.

Thank you to our intrepid agent, Liz Parker, who hustles for us every day and who's believed in us since she first learned about us way back in season one of By the Book. Liz, we so appreciate all you've done to turn our book-writing dreams into book-writing realities, and for always believing we're worthy of going further and reaching higher.

Thank you to Cassie Jones, our brilliant and patient editor at William Morrow, who helps us to do our best work, always with good cheer and a level of organization that borders on nutty. Cassie, we are so grateful to you, as well as everyone on your hardworking team—from the talented people who designed our cover to the group that makes sure we're on readers' radars.

Huge thanks to all the producers who've worked tirelessly on By the Book and our other projects. Among them, our founding producer, Cameron Drews, whose insights and story instincts set a high bar for everyone to follow; Nora Ritchie, who bravely and brilliantly took the baton, and elevated us to new heights; Casey Holford, who helps us sound like audio angels; and Lindsey Kratochwill, the founding producer/writer/all-around superstar of We Love You (And So Can You). Thanks also to everyone at Panoply and Stitcher who's believed in us and supported us in our shared podcasting endeavors: Laura Mayer, Mia Lobel, and Chris Bannon, to name just a few.

And, of course, thank you to our friends and families, who've supported our dreams, helped us through our tough moments, and allowed us to record conversations with them even when we're all at our worst. First among them: my husband, Dean, who offers me the wisest advice, always. Dean, thank you for eternally being in my corner and never being judgmental. I learn, every day, to be a better person, through your support, love, and good example. And second, but not far behind: Brad. Brad, the joy and kindness you bring to By the Book and to Jolenta are gifts to all who love you both, including me. Thank you for your infinite patience and good sense of humor. In my book, you and Dean equally share the title America's Favorite Husband.

Always and forever, thank you to my beloved Nanna and mother. In all I do, I hope to do you proud.

Last but not least, thank you to every listener who's helped make our shows the successes that they are. Your stories, your questions, your criticisms, and above all, your support for us and our work are appreciated beyond measure. Thank you for letting us share our lives with you and thank you for sharing your lives with us.

INDEX